THE
GITA SECRET

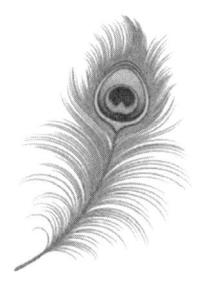

THE GITA SECRET

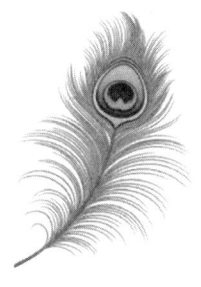

Ravi Kapur

The Gita Secret
By Ravi Kapur

ISBN 978-93-90095-46-9

First Published in 2021

Copyright © RAVI KAPUR

All rights reserved. No part of this publication may be reproduced, stored in a retrieval system, or transmitted in any form or by any means, electronic, mechanical, photocopying, recording or otherwise, without the prior written permission of the Publisher.

Disclaimer: This is a work of fiction and any resemblance to any person living or otherwise is purely co-incidental.

Published by
THIRD EYE
An imprint of
PENTAGON PRESS LLP
206, Peacock Lane, Shahpur Jat
New Delhi-110049
Phones: 011-64706243, 26491568
Telefax: 011-26490600
email: rajan@pentagonpress.in
website: www.pentagonpress.in

Printed at Aegean Offset Printers, Greater Noida, U.P.

*Dedicated to
my precious papa...*

Contents

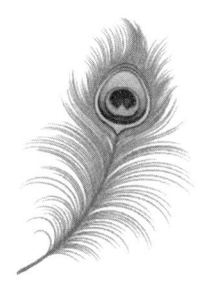

	Acknowledgement	*ix*
	A Word of Thanks	*xi*
	Prologue	*xiii*
1	DESTINY AT WORK	1
2	THE SECRET CHAPTER	10
3	THE STRATEGIC SUMMIT	18
4	DOUBLE DIPLOMACY	27
5	KARMIC CONNECTION	33
6	SCIENCE IN SCRIPTURES	39
7	THE DIVINE VISION	43
8	EMOTIONAL BONDS	52
9	THE SENSUOUS WORLD	55
10	A TRYST WITH TERROR	61
11	THE EVIL ENCOUNTER	71

12	THE BREAKTHROUGH	77
13	UNITY IN DIVERSITY	83
14	THE MENTAL MIRACLE	89
15	TYING LOOSE ENDS	95
16	THE CRYPTIC CONTACT	101
17	GATEWAY TO INFINITY	106
18	THE DOUBLE AGENT	112
19	TECHNO-SPIRITUALITY	118
20	EUREKA	125
21	THE LORD'S LEELA	131
22	THE REVELATION	137
23	GOOD - THE ULTIMATE WINNER	143
24	THE TENTH AVATAR	150
25	TRANSCENDENCE	155
	EPILOGUE	158

Acknowledgement

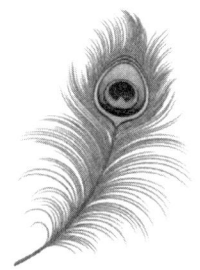

I am deeply grateful for the valuable inputs from my teenage grandson Aaditya Gandhi, top winner twice of the Emirates Airlines Litfest short story competition (Dubai) and whose awarded works have been proudly published by 'The Oxford University Press'.

A Word of Thanks

To my dear wife Neelam for patiently hearing me out and giving invaluable suggestions that have given final shape to this book.

To my dear daughter, Puja Gandhi, whose determination and hard work I truly admire, for firmly persuading me to become an author in my late forties.

To my dear son-in-law Akash Gandhi for his inputs on drones.

To my dear grand-daughter Aditi Gandhi for keeping me pepped up during the writing of this book.

AND

A very special thanks to my dear son Gautam Kapur, a true Karmyogi, for being an inspiration in my life.

Prologue

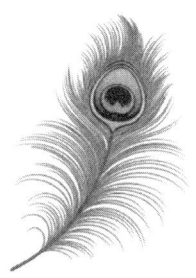

The barren battlefield would soon be bathed in blood as the two armies face each other menacingly. The sky reverberates with a sense of impending doom. He knows the futility of war and yet it must be fought. Somebody dear needs to be convinced, somebody who at that same moment is kneeling before him seeking the truth. The moment has arrived. Up goes his right hand forefinger pin-pointed towards the kneeling brain. The invisible laser-aura emerges from the blessing hand shattering bang on the gap between the seeker's two eyes to penetrate deep inside, instantly activating the target.

The seeker is jolted into another dimension swiftly sailing through a vast vortex of an endless space-time continuum, where all is one and one is all. A pulsating cosmic form engulfing the entire creation and dissolving ego in a euphoric ecstasy all morphed out of pure potential.

The infinite revelation is momentary but complete. As the kneeling eyes open all they can see is a shining peacock feather adorning their mentor's brow....

1

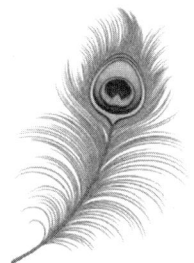

Destiny at Work

Secrets never survive. A stolen pleasure may grant momentary ecstasy but snatch a lifetime of joy. He learnt it the hard way reluctantly relenting to the harsh truth that self-change is a locked door that can be only opened from inside. The tragedy of life is that it is only lived once and lessons learnt must hit the battleground instantly. He tried hard and failed. He tried harder. Succeeded.

Adam's thoughts were zipped as Parvati, his Director of News, pushed open his thick office glass door adorned by the brass letters 'Chairman'. Managing the multi-million global corporate sitting in his Office at the top floor of the tallest structure in the world was no joke but the thirty year old Adonis like Media Baron did it with ease and aplomb. The real challenge was managing himself. As the intelligent oriental beauty in her late twenties pulled up the red leather chair opposite him, he pretended to give her a cursory look while absorbing her whole being and was floored as always. She killed with her intense looks, her mascara sharp eye lashes slashing his jugular. It was her tangy accent that brought him back to life as she addressed him by his first name as she had been instructed on the day she had joined his organization a month earlier. There was breaking news. The Nobel peace prize for the year had just been announced and surprisingly the recipient was an Indian neurologist Dr. Roy who had done pioneering research on the human brain's capacity for inducing peace including self-peace for the last 2 decades and reached amazing conclusions. The award ceremony was in two days at Stockholm and needed top coverage. It would also be attended by the Lama. The previous incumbent. Parvati was immediately asked to personally head the news team from 'Global Media Inc.' and travel in the Chairman's personal plane to Stockholm. As she got up to leave, a short closing comment from Adam that he might join her, caught her off guard. She had just glanced at the mischievous gleam in his blue eyes as she left.

Two days later, the Chairman's personal plane with the large corporate red logo took off exactly for Stockholm. Red was his color. On board was Parvati, her two new team members and Adam Gore, the Chairman himself. It was to be a one day European sojourn. The pre-award glittering dinner was on tonight to be followed by the actual one hour presentation ceremony the next morning. Included in the one day was spending a night at the luxury suite at the Stockholm Sheraton for the chairman with normal rooms for others. Adam certainly chose the best. What was uncertain was whether he would have company in the most luxurious suite. Only time would tell. Of course in Adam's case it would rather be him telling time what was coming. A tingling personal hope always made him even more work efficient. Seated next to Parvati he was already short listing the vital aspects of the coming event coverage even as his supple fingers gilded momentarily on hers. She humoured him as her mind was racing ahead to future possibilities. She was sure of one thing. hat she would never be a one-night partner to anybody, however high and mighty he may be. She was a one man woman and would wait for her Mr. Right. Of course she knew of Adam's freaky flirtatious reputation but if he was to be her Mr. Right, all that would have to change slowly but completely. Of that she was sure. She would show patience. The journey was nice and short and soon they checked in at the Sheraton well in time for the evening high dinner function. The Sheraton was the best in town with a stunning view of the old town and the city hall, fusing the old with the new. The warm ambience seemed to welcome them with open arms. A short siesta before the exotic evening soon to be ushered in Parvati felt cool and relaxed. As she slipped into her black formal dress she paused in front of the crystal crafted wall-mirror as she deftly put on her diamond tiara.

She questioned Was she in Love?.

The lemon-grass aroma filled the ambience of the massage room which was right next to the fitness centre on the first floor of the Sheraton. Adam had sacrificed his siesta to enjoy the much recommended aromatherapy massage at the hotel and he was rather liking it since he had combined it with a semi-siesta of sorts. The Swedish lady masseur,

Myra, was adept at her work, touching the exact nerve centres meant to release relaxation. He knew she was eyeing his rather fit athletic almost nude body but he had better fantasies to drown in. He had this self-irritating habit of falling asleep midway between a massage but today he was alert. Alert because he was totally relishing the fantastic fantasy of Parvati being his masseur. Tonight after the ballroom dinner...he would go for the kill. After all that was the sole purpose of making this trip. Little was he aware that destiny had a higher plan.

The soft waltz music marathon took a turn for a swift jog of jungle drums and he was saved from slumber. The massage was over but the sensuous climax to his fantasy would always remain locked in the secret chambers of his erratic psyche to be reclaimed as and when required. It had been erratic ever since his puberty years when he had lost his darling mom to cancer. A boarding education, an even harsher father and then the final inheritance of the chairmanship of the global mega media corporate had all been instigators to his erratic psyche now hideously hidden in the deep dark dungeon of his subconscious surreality. He dreaded loneliness. Anyways he had proved the Pandits wrong by his awesome acumen at taking Global Media Inc. to the numero uno positioning in the media world. He was the undisputed leader and master of his worldly profession but alas! a mere slave of his own personal bondage. But now there was hope or so he had thought. Parvati had entered.

A persistent but gentle knock on the mahogany door of his suite acted as an alarm. Time to formally dress up and go down. The black and satin 3 piece suit with the gold chained watch complimented his aristocracy and soon he was dancing to a timeless symphony. His feet were firmly pivoting on the glazed wooden dance floor but his mind was somewhere else, looking down with amazement at the elegant black gown and diamond tiara of his stunningly beautiful waltz partner. They hit off well on the dance floor he could see as in the boardroom, but bedroom matters remained enigmatic. Of course, he had never let a future apprehension spoil a present pleasure and the policy had paid off well as it was doing now. Mother would have been ecstatic tonight at the duo dancing away but in his deep core he knew that life with a mate would always be a threesome...mom would always be around. The cheering halted the music as the chairman of the awards committee entered. A toast for the winner ensued.

Parvati had been amazed at her own flexibility during the electric evening. He had bowed humbly and asked for a dance and she had relented after a momentary hesitation. He had dared to kiss her brow during a pivot in the waltz and she had not even murmured a symbolic protest and now she was holding long crystal champagne glasses on a private gallery moon lighting with someone she had hardly met. Her single-parent mom back in Dubai would shudder and shrug violently if she came to know. Life is built up on moments and some of them are imprisoning and this was one of them for her as she entered his exclusive penthouse suite where she remained till the wee hours of the morning.

That whole night Adam and Parvati did not make love. They cried.

Sometimes an arduous wait for pleasure fizzles out when the opportunity is suddenly granted. That night at the penthouse of the Sheraton something more happened. The temporary surge towards mutual physical pleasures seemed to be inexplicably distilled into a pure platonic platform of mutual musings of two successful but unhappy lives. Two minds ripped of all secrets merged as tears trickled down four eyes. The dawn realized that they had revealed their naked souls to each other and had no regrets in either but instead had instilled a potent personal bond besides the professional that would soon be formalised, no doubt. It was Adam who broke the long silence by two words as he glanced at his pure gold watch that had been specially crafted for him:

"Good morning..."

Parvati did not answer but snuggled closer on the king size bed. Adam loved king size things. She planted a sensuous long lip to lip transfusion of love. He hugged her torso tight as fabrics were ripping off to reveal beautiful bodies immaculately intertwined. She was barely breathing, drowned in the large loving eyes on a fair soft face with a broadish jawline, the mole on the side cheek and the flirting dimple below the lower lip. The receding hairline lent a mature sexuality she felt as his temporary paunch stood out. He combined the ravishing body of his British father with the ethnic features of his Indian mom. His roving eyes seemed riveted on her nippled toppings even as his slender fingers gently groped towards them sweetly stroking them to spring them back from a long slumber. She was flooded inside. He had his gadgets handy to make the encounter memorable for her and it was. The hunting game was over. He had got the best. No more fun-filled evenings in London with ex-girlfriends. Now total loyalty, trust and care for his life love. Entering his thirties must bring maturity and one day he would no doubt like his kids to look up to him not as a flirt but as a man of character. He would accept Parvati lovingly as she was, always be by her side and be someone she could always depend upon, come what may. He knew he would never cheat on her in thought, word and deed. The mere thought of total commitment to one person gave him a sense of personal security and stability and in one stroke all past sins were self-forgiven. He was enough. On that Swedish dawn, Adam had found his one and only soul mate.

It was at the lounge buffet, the very next day, over a Danish croissant that he proposed. She pleaded for time as he smiled and relented. A jingle on his custom mader Rolex reminded him of the presentation ceremony as both rushed to their rooms to be formally attired. As she got into a swarovski studded cream side slit gown and a high neck that thankfully hid the love bite he had planted last night, she was smugly patting herself on the back for not saying yes immediately. Men must be made to wait. Of course, it was entirely another matter that for her the self-imposed waiting period would be an anxious interlude asdeep inside she had already whispered Yes. She knew how to bring a swift culmination to the irritating but vital brief exile.

He knew it too.

Parvati deftly clicked open the red elongated case to extract her mom's exquisitely carved diamond bracelet now gifted to her with love. It had carried special memories her mom had remarked as she had placed the red case in her hands on her last birthday and had added that it would bring a special one into her life soon. It had. As Parvati slipped her slender fingers through it a gentle double knock on the door made her instantly utter:

"Enter"

The sturdy doorway slid open to reveal Adam approaching her slowly, a mischievous smile almost breaking free on the handsome face. She was thinking. Why in the name of heavens above was this man here at this time when they were, in any case ,meeting for the ceremony. Her thoughts were interrupted by his cool voice:

"May I enter".

Her answer was logical:

"You already have".

They both giggled as he delicately held her in his arms. A kiss on her brow made her blush as he stuttered:

"I shall always love you..."

It was then that it happened. There he was down on his knees and with a solitaire ring asking her to marry him. It was the passion in the word he added that made it clear to her that he wanted an immediate answer. He pleaded:

"Please..."

There was no option left as she said:

"Yes, my darling."

The hug that followed the slipping on the ring seemed eternal. Yesterday she came to the Sheraton single. Today she will enter the Nobel presentation hall arm in arm with her fiancé. On that exotic evening, destiny had delivered. Two soul mates had become one.

2

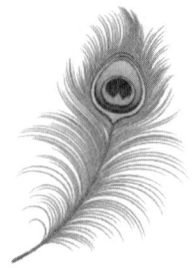

THE SECRET CHAPTER

Gopal was in his teens when his grandpa started teaching him the nuances of astrology in their ancestral home in Kurukshetra, India where ages ago the Mahabharata battle was fought. Gopal was a direct descendant of Pandit Ved Vyas who authored the Gita. A handsome man of 25 with aquiline features, Gopal, still remembered how his grandfather had opened up a new world before him when he started teaching astrology to his then teenage grandson. The impact of planetary positions at the time of birth of a person on his entire life was truly perplexing but appeared largely correct given the case studies put before Gopal by his teacher. There were so many permutations with the numerous planets and the various houses in a natal chart that only experience or focused study would bring excellence in an astrologer. Total dedication was required, Gopal knew that. And Gopal was dedicated

On a dawn in December, many years ago, just before his demise his grandfather in gasping whispers had revealed a family secret to Gopal's father. On the 41st day after grandpa's death, Gopal's father summoned him and spoke thus:

"Gopu, listen carefully now. When you will be 25 years old, some people will come to visit you seeking something vital which needs to be released to humanity and for which our family has acted as secret custodians down the ages ever since our ancestor wrote the Gita. This epic has given an awesome wisdom to mankind through its eighteen chapters but today I reveal to you a secret that has travelled down our generations.

There is a 19th chapter of the Gita which was withheld by Ved Vyas Ji at Krishna's instructions as the human race was not ready yet. It was to be revealed when the time came to mark the advent of Satyuga. Preserved on barks, papyrus and paper, handed down from generation to generation, sworn to secrecy, the time is soon to come for its release. You are the lucky one Gopal who is to hand it over to the seekers who will approach you around your 25th birthday."

There is a pause as the speaker gulps some water from a copper tumbler to drench his parched throat. Gopal's mind is in a whirlpool as he finds himself murmuring up.

"Where is this secret chapter, dear father ?"

His dad resumed speaking, pointing to an iron safe embedded in the east wall of the room .

"In there you will find a red cloth in which the writing is preserved. Here is the key. I pass it on to you for my astrology tells me I shall be no more in one year...

Gopal had a final question as he wiped a solitary tear:

"How will I know the seekers are genuine"

Quick came the answer:

"You will be able to identify them through the fact that one of them will be a man of brain-science..."

Gopal's ears were listening intently but his mind was totally intruded by a penetrating query:

'What was in the Gita's secret 19th Chapter'.

That night Gopal could not sleep. There are moments when one knows that one stands at a vital cross road engrossed between the past and future and curiously cogitating on one's own life pathway. The past had trained him perfectly in the art of astrology thanks to his grandpa.

It had also shaped him into what he believed was a good human being, thanks to his mom. She had left him for her heavenly abode when he had barely entered his teens but her impact on him had gained ground with each passing year. Love is the biggest network connecting humans she used to remind him often and her teachings had become part of his genetic grounding. Today, he thought of her as a spark of divinity empowering him to do good. His quest for a life with a purpose seemed closer than ever before. The revelation about the 19th chapter and his impending role in its transmission to humanity seemed exceedingly exciting, even as he stumbled towards slumber. The final impression on his mind before slipping into the mystic void called sleep was a hazy image of the nude torso of his teenage friend as they bathed together on the banks of the holy Ganges.

Thunderous applause greeted Dr. Laik K Roy as he received the Nobel. A middle aged man, with greying hair scattered across his scalp, merging almost seamlessly with black with deep brown eyes finely complementing his wise look. This was a pinnacle moment for the esteemed neurologist as his work of decades was being recognized finally.

It was during the high breakfast buffet when Dr. Roy was closeted with the Lama that Adam who knew them earlier in his capacity as a media baron, joined in accompanied by Parvati.

The exchange of pleasantries over it was the Lama who suddenly gestured the foursome towards a secluded corner of the hall and lowered his tone as he spoke to them in almost hushed tones:

"Roy, I have an urgent request to make to you and it is good that Adam and his associates are with us.

The ascent of the human race has been steady but sometimes a present gift of insight from the past can unfold awesome progress for the future. However such a process requires a dedicated and brilliant human mind and today I have found one. Dr. Roy may I request you along with Adam and Parvati to meet me in my hotel room in an hour's time. It is my earnest desire to pass on a stupendous baton to you that may well change the future evolution of the human race. Are all of you ready?"

The Lama gasped for breath as he hopefully looked at the three dazed faces looking for their approval to meet up in his room shortly. It was Dr. Roy who was the first to respond to the Lama in ochre robes:

"Done. We shall all be there and I confidently answer for all of us as we deem it a great honour coming from your Holiness."

Adam and Parvati nodded enthusiastically as the Lama took leave. They would all assemble at the agreed place and time. Parvati was aware of an eerie expectancy of the coming unfolding of events that only time would tell.

It was exactly one hour later as the cuckoo clock chirped that three curious beings entered the Lama's room.

He welcomed them and as they sipped lemon green tea the holy man had an amazing true tale to tell:

"Friends, as you are aware, due to the Chinese advance in Tibet, I had to flee to India and a lot of luggage including some very old trunks were shifted to our capital in exile near Dharamshala. Recently an ancient scroll came into my possession from one of the trunks that remained unopened.

It was on an unknown bark pulped into the form of a thick paper with ancient red fluid ink like writing in an ancient dialect of Sanskrit language. What is written in the scroll which I have translated into English will astound you..."

The lama's voice trailed into a mystic silence as the people around him moved closer. Parvati suddenly erupted:

"Holiness, where is the scroll now?"

The lama's reply was instant:

"Here...Friends I have got the original scroll with its translation right here and now in this room..."

As he said these words, The holy man took out a small leather bag from under his chair and unzipped it took out an old parchment like scroll with an A4 size bond paper with typed English words on it. He proceeded to read from the sheet:

"I, Lobsang Rampa, am hereby recording a statement made by my close friend Jaitly Sharma made by him on the day he breathed his last breath. I am reproducing Jaitly's last words here under:

I, Jaitly Sharma, am a direct descendant of Pandit Ved Vyas who wrote the Hindu epic The Gita including the Mahabharata, which records the battle of Kurukshetra and the teachings of Lord Krishna to Arjuna. The Gita has 18 chapters. I have known a family secret handed down by word of mouth over the generations whereby Ved Vyas Ji had ordained that he had written a secret chapter of the Gita (The 19th chapter), which is still to be revealed to man when the appropriate time comes as per Krishna's instructions.

This chapter contained the secret knowledge forming the doorway to man's evolution to a higher level. The time will come in kaliyuga and a learned man will come in the field of human brain study to bring this secret knowledge in practical form for usage by humanity. Pandit Ved Vyas hereby gives a clue as to how the secret Gita chapter has to be hunted for by this learned man of brain sciences. Go to the land of the Mahabharata battleground and seek out my i.e. Ved Vyas' youngest descendant of that age. Ved Vyas Ji urges the man of brain sciences: Please do this service to humanity. Please. I, Jaitly Sharma, close my statement here. God bless the people reading it now including the learned man of the brain—sciences..."

The Lama stopped reading as the words on the sheet had ended.

Dr. Roy was lost in deep introspection. How could an ancient document have known that a man of brain sciences would be present at the time of the document reading was amazing. Something inside his core was urging him to take the karmic leap.

Dr. Roy broke the momentary tense silence:

"Holiness, I am ready..."

The Lama embraced Dr. Roy as he spoke up:

"I knew you would take up the challenge for the future of mankind. And may I also request Adam to depute dear Parvati to assist Dr. Roy in this pilgrimage as a media representative if she graciously agrees."

Adam was quick to affirm and so was Parvati.

A strong inexplicable bond had evolved among the foursome and Parvati knew that strong forces of destiny were now at work. It was decided that Dr. Roy and Parvati would leave for India straightaway in pursuit of the secret chapter

19 of the Gita and Adam would return to Dubai.

The Lama would reach Dharamshala to his capital in exile. They would all take to different directions physically now but their mental or rather spiritual destination was slowly converging. It seemed as if the past was ripping open the present to give birth to an amazing future for the human race.

As Dr. Roy was alone in his room; there was in him a motley of emotions mixing up to form a curious cocktail. Euphoria garnished with tense excitement at looming possibilities ultimately gave way to past moments where he recalled his loving parents urging him to work hard to gain excellence. He knew that they knew about his powerful potential, somewhat obstacled by his laziness. College education blossomed into post-graduation in the subject of his fantasy. The human mind had always intrigued him and had to be unraveled not only at the physical level but much more beyond. The Lama's assignment had opened up that subconscious challenge in him to reach out to infinity itself as that was what the human mind was the gateway to. Yes, he would do it and ultimately fulfill the purpose of his life. He knew that. What he did not know was that in achieving his life's mission he would be redeeming someone's pledge to humanity made millennia ago.

3

THE STRATEGIC SUMMIT

China with its 1.38 billion population was the numero uno nation as far as human resources were concerned. What was surprising was that till recently it was also the fastest growing economy in the world with about a 10 per cent growth rate. The disturbing feature was political. The leaders of this so-called dragon nation had hardly hidden their future ambitions to rule the world. To achieve this end all means were justified and therein lay the dangerous threat to the other peaceful nations in the contemporary world order.

Beijing's International Airport was said to be the world's second largest in terms of traffic as was evident as the Emirates Airways flight landed there right on time from Dubai. It was carrying a VIP passenger Begum Noor Bano, the chairperson of the United Nations Peace Foundation (UNPF), an apex active arm of the United Nations that sought to promote global peace and development through dynamic communication and catalytic diplomatic action among the members of the crucial security council. If the UNPF was active, its Chairperson was pro-active as her current international tour clearly indicated. She would be personally deliberating with the top leadership of China, India, America and Russia, in that order, before returning to her headquarters at Dubai.

A fierce gaze was the initial trademark of Begum Bano, a chiseled face- the second and a determination to bring to life her ideal dream, the third. It would almost appear as if she had conspired to atone for all of humanity's follies, with the way she held herself aloof and presented herself almost as if she was always meant to bring peace to the globe. A UN peace ambassador she travelled across the world from one nation to another to solve international disputes and promote peace and development. No doubt her task was strenuous due to the contemporary ambience of conflict around the world, yet she appeared victorious if only for temporary periods of time. Her somewhat tragic past imbibed her with a sense of courage only seen in those who faced numerous hardships yet succeeded and this left her determined to ensure she could work for a gratified future for others given her willingness for personal sacrifice.

Zhongnanhai housed the headquarters of The Communist party of The people's republic of China and this is where Begum Bano was being escorted to by China's Culture Minister, Madam Ching Lee, a delicate lady with beauty of body and mind as per the Begum's powerful intuitions, that became especially energized on her foreign jaunts, could catch. As the black limousine entered the main gates of their destination Madam Lee took The Begum's hand in hers and hoped they would meet again.

A strong bond had been born between the two during the short drive from the Airport. Like minds merge fast.

The official discussions with The Top leader of China, Chairman Zing Tse was just that—official, dry and dismal. The Begum could sense a hidden hostility to concepts like international communication, disarmament and aid for underdeveloped nations. It was clear that China wanted to rule the world one day and would adopt all means to reach that dominant superpower status. The curt cup of tea over, the meeting ended abruptly as the Chairman was urgently required elsewhere. Madam Lee appeared out of seemingly nowhere to escort Begum once again to her hotel for her overnight stay before her departure for India the next morning. The Chinese minister broke the silence as they started the drive towards the Hotel Hilton.

"So we meet again..."

The two ladies smiled as Begum Bano deftly adjusted her grey gown and replied:

"It has been a pleasure to have met you Madam...My inner being tells me you are a lady of peace and we will be always working in unison towards that mission..."

The Chinese lady nodded in affirmation just as the Limousine drove into the Hilton porch where the General manager was duly present to escort The Chairperson of The UNPD to her suite on the top floor. That night as Begum

Bano enjoyed the distant lights of Beijing from her hotel balcony, mixed feelings prevailed in her.

The meeting with Chairman Zing had been most disappointing and dark. However as is said every dark cloud has a silver lining. In this scenario the silver lining to the darkness had a name.

It was called Madam Ching Lee.

Ever since Adam Gore had reached back to Dubai from the Nobel ceremony he had been feeling lost and restless. He knew the reason but was trying hard not to admit it to himself. Egos die hard but it is a harsh fact that one cannot lie to oneself. In the deepest depth of his being Adam was aware of the cause for his turmoil. He was missing Parvati. It was a first time feeling for him to be experiencing as he tossed from one side of his king size bed to the other and finally looked at the time on his gold mobile to see that it was 5 A.M. in Dubai which meant 6/30 A.M. in India. Impulsively he pressed her number hoping against hope that she would be up. Unfortunately she was still sleeping.

The bell seemed to ring for eternity before her tangy voice whispered the two words he wanted to hear:

"Love you."

He replied by sending her an e-kiss by imprinting his sensuous lips on the mobile screen before starting the long and loving verbal chat in which she promised to update him professionally later in the day. Her concluding remark made him wince as she said:

"Bye for now darling...and be a good boy in my absence...see you soon."

The remark was casual but the relationship with the person from whom it came was not. It sent an urgent signal into the core of Adam's being that now he had to change drastically.

No more flings of the flesh, no more freaky flirtations and strictly no more one-night stances for sure. Game Over. It would be difficult but he knew he could do it as the reason for motivating the change was compelling. Parvati had entered his life surreptitiously overshadowing his whole being. It was like a bright light had been put on and banished the dark side of his personality forever. A new Adam, adamant as ever ,had been born and he wanted to change towards his new role as a single woman man.

The Burj Khalifa, the highest man made structure on the globe seemed to look down benevolently on the Dubai mall much below along with a string of residential buildings including 29, Boulevard the most recent one. Sitting in his plush office on the top floor of The Burj had always been an empowering experience for The Chairman of 'Global Media Inc.' and more so on that somewhat cloudy morning when exciting international media events were afoot. In his role of an uncrowned King of the media world Adam knew the pulse of the globe and its top leaders. Only a couple of days ago he had been alerted about a vital but clandestine international event coming up shortly. Confidential powerful sources had confided with Adam that the leaders of the two top nations namely America and Russia would be having a secret summit at an undisclosed destination soon to forge a united anti-China diplomatic front to counter the dragon nation's growing power.

The implications of such an event were to say the least awesome. In the global scenario of the day, the coming together of the two strong nations would change power equations drastically. The resulting ramifications would be amazing. It was a challenge Adam just had to take up. He desperately wanted to cover the secret summit and wanted Intel on the time and place of the summit but had not succeeded so far as all his usual sources had failed to dig up anything.

Only a final very top source remained—as potentially powerful and as it was personally proximate to him. He pressed an unlisted number to connect to this source.

At that very moment in response to his pressing, a mobile bell started jingling in a top floor suite of Hotel Hilton in Beijing. The Begum said that she too had an inkling but would confirm after her meeting with the American and Russian Presidents.

The moment Adam's inside info on the secret summit was confirmed by the Begum, whom he had always admired as a diplomat and more recently as his future mom in law, he was jolted into action mode. He punched a single digit on his red intercom and gave some urgent instructions. He would now be able to infiltrate inside the private villa in Switzerland where the two top leaders would be meeting later that day. Once he got the city name, finding the exact venue was child's play, given his resources. Money was power and power based on knowledge was clout. The instructions over, he closed his eyes for a split second. Smug satisfaction.

When he re-opened his eyes he could see knocking on his glass cabin door was a new Pakistani girl he had hired as head of Administration. His nod made her glide in as he ogled her nonchalantly. Habits die hard but he had drawn a line for self-discipline ever since the moment his ring had been accepted and had been able to honour it. Appreciating beauty only by looking...nothing more. The lady was putting in a personal request for a short leave and left his cabin discreetly the moment it was rejected. The private hotline was flashing and he picked up the receiver instantly as he knew this was important. Needful arrangements had been completed to listen in to the summit and Adam would be able to hear the secret verbal telecast meant for his ears only. He would have to reach home within half an hour to be able to receive the same on a unique frequency. He immediately got up to leave.

The first sound that reached Adam's ears as he switched on was the translator who was responding on behalf of the Russian leader to the American President's greetings.

And then the acoustics went dead for the next 10 crucial minutes. Sometimes all efforts and finesse become futile despite best efforts. Adam was feeling helpless not being able to hear the crucial talk of the two most important men on the globe. He was reminded of the verse in The Gita that the right of action was a man's but not the fruits of action. Then all of a sudden the silence ended. The clinking of spoons rotating inside coffee cups broke the irritating interruption as The Chairman of Global Media Inc. strained his ears to make sense of the barely audible conversation that appeared to be tingling with tension as it seemed to be drawing to a close. Adam clearly heard President Taylor congratulate the suave head of the Russian Confederation, President Prestov on their just signing the secret pact for a united front against China. Adam heard the words and seemed to freeze instantly. It was exactly at that moment that the system went dead.

In a world where the Cold War and non-alignment eras were dead and replaced by a tripartite emergence of three super powers namely America, Russia and China, the coming together of two of them to isolate the third one was to say the least a paradigm shift in the global scenario. To the average man on the street it may be like an enigma of sorts but to the seasoned player in the global media order, the significance was extremely deep.

Henceforth this secret knowledge that Adam had just acquired would be critical for any contemporary assessment of global affairs.

Of course this would never have been possible without the help of the one and only Begum Bano. He looked forward to her association as a professional partnership coupled with the strong personal bond as Parvati's mother.

Adam was tingling with power as now he was privy to something only a handful of humans knew.

Russia and America had just signed a secret pact to forge a united anti-China front—a fact that would have awesome global implications henceforth.

4

DOUBLE DIPLOMACY

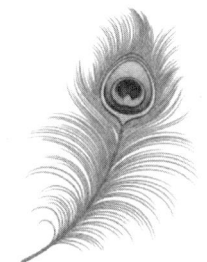

Begum Bano looked gracefully glamorous despite her mid-fifties in her pastel blue gown as she boarded the flight to Washington. As per her planned itinerary, Delhi would have been her next stop but an emergency change to one meet with the President of the United States as per his sudden request made her amend her travel plans. Delhi visit would now come up last after her Moscow sojourn While in the USA she would also be inaugurating a peace conference during a one-day visit to New York.

It was a few months back that she had last met the American President at an International conference on environment and global warming at Paris. She had found him to be a very warm and reasonable man ready to act for global welfare. The encounter had encouraged her to put in a request for a hefty donation for global good. She was looking forward to the vital meeting.

On the flight to Washington, the Begum was engrossed in reading about America and the American President.

President Frederick W. Taylor intrigued her. A conservative to the core he was trying to showcase himself as a dynamic futuristic liberal or so she thought. The plus point was that he was basically peace loving and detested violence more so in the global arena. She sincerely hoped that their Oval Office meeting would click and she would get his approval for a hefty donation to The UNPF. Dollars still mattered.

A few hours later she was ushered into the legendary Oval Office at the White House with its plush green lawns outside. It was the first time that The Begum was visiting the famous Oval room at the White House, the most powerful desk right in front of her.

The intricate carving on the desk held her attention momentarily even as POTUS got up from his desk to welcome her. There was a brief eye contact between them, as Bano had wanted. President Taylor immaculate in his blue pinstripe suit looked much younger than his late fifties as he warmly addressed her:

"Delighted to see you Madam...and sorry for the last minute change in the itinerary. Something very urgent came up and I have to travel early tomorrow morning even though it's just for a day."

Begum Bano shook his extended hands delicately, taking in the softness and warmth. A mere handshake conveyed a lot ,consequent to her developing the art of handshake reading. She knew now that she could do business with Frederick as she verbally responded:

"No problems Sir...it has always been a personal as well

as a professional pleasure to meet you..."

The dedicated duo then settled down to a long chat on the international scenario including the stealthily growing Chinese clout that had somewhat ominous global implications. As China was mentioned The President made a sudden brief off the cuff remark that made Bano sit up as she heard his unusually low voice mutter:

"Err...we will be doing something about this..."

His voice trailed off as he seemed to suddenly shut his mouth for fear of revealing more. The awkward silence was broken by the arrival of aromatic black coffee over which the Begum was able deftly to get the Presidential approval for the generous dollars grant. The coffee session over, they then resumed their dialogue as she briefed him on the latest UNPF initiatives to promote World Peace and got a very positive response in contrast to that of The Chinese leader.

Just as she was about to get up, the hotline came alive with sharp shrieks.

The President instantly picked it up and seemed to be listening intently for a few seconds before speaking up in hushed tones:

"It is confirmed then...10 A.M. tomorrow at Lausanne..."

Begum Bano had extra sharp ears and just as the Hotline clicked shut she distinctly heard a flying subdued single word echo: 'dashvidania'...

A quick handshake and she was out of the White House and her chaperoned limousine was driving her to her

Washington hotel. She had still to draft her speech for the peace conference at New York tomorrow but before that she had to do something urgent ASAP. A crucial info had come to her in the Oval Office...President Taylor was meeting someone very important at Lausanne tomorrow morning. She was reminded of Taylor's cryptic remark about something being done about China and could make out that tomorrow's meeting was crucial. Who was the person who would be secretly meeting Frederick tomorrow? The crucial clue to this puzzle lay in the single word she had heard coming from the speaker at the other end of the Hotline. Dashvidania is a Russian word meaning We will meet again. My God...the sudden realization hit her. The Presidents of the two most powerful nations were having a secret anti-China summit tomorrow. She just had to convey this to someone at this very instant.

The limousine turned towards Main Avenue as Begum Bano dialed and listed a number on her mobile. A matter of fact tense voice spoke up at the other end immediately. It was Adam Gore.

The flight to Moscow from New York was on time and Begum Bano felt relaxed during the journey after her hectic New York one day schedule. Her inauguration speech at the peace conference had gone off well and she now looked forward to meeting the Russian President. Moscow on the Moskva River in western Russia is the nation's cosmopolitan capital. Its historic core is the Kremlin that is home to the President.

President Mikhail Prestov was an intelligent and ambitious leader in his mid-forties whose handsome visage despite the receding hairline hid his cruel KGB past rather well. The Begum knew that his level of commitment to peace lay somewhere between that of The Chinese and The American leaders. Prestov had a murky past as the KGB head and there was talk of political murders on his way to the top. He had no family and had never married making him presumably the least vulnerable to blackmail by his opponents. Bano knew the psychological set up of the man having met him twice earlier including one to one. She was a student of human psyche and during her private meeting with Prestov in the UNO had observed that he was prone to use the word I in preference to We. Such persons were open to flattery. The Begum knew that he could go either way and needed deft diplomatic handling to convince him that on the pathway to peace lay his nations and his own personal triumph. Personal triumph was the crucial word. Bano had plans to tap Prestov's ego to accomplish global goals.

Diplomacy, it was said, was the art of getting what one wants from others, making them think that it is what they want themselves. The Begum had over the years evolved herself as an adept diplomat and felt rather smug about it.

As Bano drove into the Kremlin, the fortified complex in the heart of Moscow, she could see the river Moscova in full swing as the Red Square made its presence felt on the eastern skyline. The handshake was vigorous but cold, typical of fence sitters. The challenge had begun as the Begum blurted:

"President Petrov, what a pleasure to be meeting you once again...but your hands are cold."

The autonomous answer provided her with the confirmation she was seeking as Petrov smiled and mumbled:

"Thanks to yesterday's Swiss weather..."

So there had been a Summit in Lausanne after all. She hoped Adam had utilized her tip off effectively. Her thoughts were curtailed as The Russian leader was lecturing on his recent peace initiatives rather egotistically. She broke in:

"Mikhail, you are a marvelous leader and the globe is proud of you."

The use of his first name was catalytic as soon and sure enough he was eating out of her hands and instantly approving the various UNPF initiatives for which The Begum wanted his approval desperately. Mission accomplished she got up to leave remarking:

"Today, President Petrov, I am fully convinced that you are a man of peace."

Mikhail thanked her profusely and his parting handshake was now vigorous and warm. The fence sitter had been won. As her black limousine drove out from the Kremlin gates her mobile rang. She glanced at the number and her heart missed a beat. It was her daughter. As she slid her delicate finger on the green line to accept the call, a chirpy voice spoke from the other end.

It was Parvati.

5

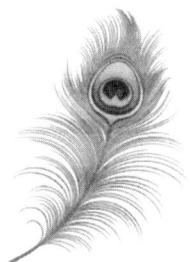

KARMIC CONNECTION

Begum Bano took the flight from Moscow to New Delhi climbing the stairs to the plane briskly. It was the final part of her current tour before flying back to her headquarters at Dubai. As the plane took off, her mind meandered through her activities in the last few days. Meeting the top leaders of the leading super powers had given her a pretty good idea about the perspectives of these nations as represented by their leaders and it had left her a bit anxious. The most worrying part was the stringent attitude of the Chinese leader who had a somewhat arrogant stance and a mistaken notion that he was all-powerful. It was the latest nuclear arsenal that China possessed that needed to be neutralized somehow to ensure world peace and stability. She now knew from Adam about the Secret American-Russian pact against China and secretly and strongly welcomed it. So far so good.

A gentle touch from the beautiful air hostess and the Begum was back in the present enjoying her mid-air meal of smoked salmon. She was looking forward to her interactions with the Indian Prime Minister. It so happened that India had a young lady as its Prime Minister who was as dynamic as she was sincere in her efforts for world peace. Dr. Lakshmi Pandit had at one time been her country's representative to the United Nations and this experience in international diplomacy was standing her in good stead. The Begum knew from her earlier interactions with Lakshmi that she could do business with her. They had shared a warm rapport right from the word go.

As the plane landed and taxied to a halt she was confident that her visit would go well. A senior minister was there at the Tarmac to receive her and the Begum was driven straight to the prime minister's house for dinner.

Dr. Pandit was there in the portico to receive her and personally escort her inside after a warm hug as she said:

"Begum a very warm welcome to India. I was looking forward to your visit."

The Begum responded with a big hug and smiled as she got in and settled on the big settee for a long chat on the contemporary international scenario.

The pre-dinner conversation lasted half an hour and the Begum could clearly identify her innermost feelings with those of the Indian leader. Peace was most important for both and both were ready to use undiplomatic means like intelligent manipulative tactics to achieve it. This was Lord Krishna's genre of diplomacy at work as in the epic Mahabharata. China had to be curtailed and Begum shared the most secret info about the pact between the two superpowers. They both expressed joy over this development and agreed to remain in touch.

It was over a typical Mughlai dinner and as Laxmi got up to personally serve her, Bano noticed how charming the Indian leader looked defying her age of 50 years. Intelligence combined with beauty at times but both combined with moral commitment of character rarely. This was it. A brief but satisfying session and in the morning Banu would fly to Dubai her professional and personal home. The final session was brief but vital as the two ladies agreed to play a proactive and coordinated role in global affairs. The Begum was well aware of the intrinsic power of India in international affairs even without the tag of a global superpower. The fact that it was led by a leader committed to peace was extremely satisfying for the Begum.

As she was getting into the car to leave for the Indira Gandhi International Airport, Laxmi handed her a gift wrapped in golden paper. Bano opened it on the way and was delighted.

It was a small marble replica of the Taj Mahal, the eternal symbol of affection and unity. The replica would occupy a prized place in the Begum's office henceforth.

It is an eerie yet peaceful experience. A vast infinite cosmic contact dynamic to the core where endings and beginnings of all there is in a constant flux of being and becoming without any boundaries of Space and Time auto converting potential into actuality and vice a versa. The experience, The experienced and the experiencer seem to merge in a singularity till the subject questions himself whether it is a dream he is going through or an access to his own subconscious that he has somehow miraculously achieved. One thing cannot be denied is that the experience is real. The experience has ended but the subconscious mind of the experiencer keeps going in a quest to comprehend the amazing reality.

Dr Roy gets up with a start with pearls of sweat adorning his brow. He looks around dazed. Ah! His eyes fall on a young figure sharing the room. Parvati. Yes. They are in Kurukshetra waiting for the morning meeting with Gopal Sharma, direct descendant of Pandit Ved Vyas. In a flash the neurologist has grasped the dream like an interlude as a gateway to what they are seeking. It was his karma that he be associated with the search for the Secret Chapter. Karma ushers in past lifetimes he knew. He had read a book titled The Sacred Secret on it by an author named Ravi Kapur. A sneeze from the Doctor and she was up wishing Good Morning and him ordering tea. A shabbily dressed boy came with two glass tumblers of tea and the duo started sipping the eye opening concoction. She went to the washroom and he was out for a stroll in the green fields. The sun was slowly peeping from the horizon accompanied by a sparrow's chirping. Dr Roy recalled the previous night's dream vividly yet a solitary part was eluding his memory. It was like chasing a shadow. A burst of fresh oxygen and he was nearly back at the hotel. He could remember holding and twirling it in his hands in the dream but about what it was he was blank. And then it happened. As he was about to push open the hotel lobby door the creature suddenly rushed across his path leaving a part of himself in his hands.

He looked down at his right hand and there it was. He was holding the same object that he had been twirling in his cosmic experience now indelibly carved on his psyche that he was slowly comprehending.

A multi-coloured peacock feather glistening radiantly in all its glory in the crimson skylight of that blessed morning in Kurukshetra.

The moment Gopal came to know that some people were coming to meet him the next morning an anticipatory thrill overtook him. His father's prediction was materialising. Events in his recent life had been tumultuous with a pair of family deaths leaving an onerous legacy to be passed on a family secret protected down the centuries and generations of Pandit Ved Vyasji's bloodline. What was to be passed on was secure in the east wall safe of his father's bedroom. The contents were secret. To whom this precious legacy was to be passed on was a big question except for a solitary clue that it would be a man of brain sciences. Gopal was cogitating on his own role and life in the coming days. That moon lit night he had answers to seek and in that quixotic quest turned to that branch of knowledge that he could trust totally.

Astrology.

It was well past midnight when all the planetary charts ready spread over the blue bedspread on which he had slept since his teenage years. The ancestral scrolls detailed the position of the planets at any given time. The real art lay in interpolating and interpreting the linkage between an individual horoscope and the universal planetary positions. His grandfather had trained him well. Earnest endeavour and dogged determination had instigated brilliance in Gopal aided by the fact that he was a science student. He was aware that he actually carried the genes of his grandfather. As the clock struck 1 am, Gopal was thinking of the scientist philosopher Eddington who had remarked that the real riddle was not the universe but the human mind. More than 2000 years before Eddington Gopal recalled another human mind, the author of the Rig Veda, who had commented that prior question as to how finite minds could comprehend infinite issues, also demanded an answer (hymn 129, book 10).

Gopal took two hours to master the charts before him. Then he got up and reverently entered his father's bedroom to pay respects to the portraits of his ancestors there. A wild impulse to read the secret chapter in the safe came and vanished. His journey had begun intertwined with The Secret Chapter he now knew. The message of the charts had jolted him. His life henceforth would pioneer as part of a group the oncoming of a new era in human affairs. He was the chosen one to pass on the family legacy to a man of brain sciences who would be knocking on his door carrying his saffron self-painted name plate the next morning. He was the fulcrum now.

The temptation to open the safe and read the secret was momentary. It was not for him to pilfer but pass on the precious legacy. In doing so he would become a part and parcel of a wisdom Tsunami that would form a vital component of Krishna's redemption promised to mankind millennia ago on the same sacred ground on which he now stood that very moment.

6

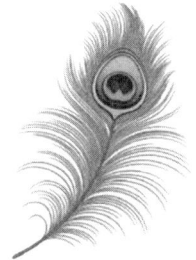

SCIENCE IN SCRIPTURES

The first impression of Kurukshetra in Parvati's mind was of heat and dust. They had landed at Indira Gandhi International Airport early in the morning and hired a cab to go to Kurukshetra by road, a journey of 3 hours. Dr. Roy was looking tired as they entered the motel where they were to stay. Parvati hoped it would be a brief stay of a couple of days praying silently for quick answers to the mystic quest that destiny had handed out to them. Of course she had gained something invaluable already even before initiating the search for the missing Gita chapter. She had gained a father figure in the shape of Dr. Roy, something that she had missed out in life till then.

A short siesta after a light continental lunch and both were googling for all Sharma's in Kurukshetra having linkage with Pandit Ved Vyas. There were five alternatives thrown up by the search engine with addresses based on self-claims of each that they were descendants of the learned author of The Gita. Dr. Roy decided to visit each to assess personally as to which one was relevant to their quest. Till nightfall they had covered 4 and rejected them. Each of the Sharma's they met were greedy and had stated their linkages on self-hollow claims without corroboration. It was dark and Dr. Roy decided to visit the last one early the next morning.

Dr. Roy made a casual remark as they were having an Indian dinner. He said:

"Dear Parvati, it has been a pleasure to have you around and may I share something...you are a daughter-like figure in my life and I thank God for this."

Both hugged and wished luck to each other for the final morning meeting.

At sharp 8am both Parvati and Dr Roy were knocking on an anciently carved wooden doorway that was opened by a young man of about 25 years immaculately dressed in a pure white kurta-pyjama, the traditional Indian dress. The sign board on the outer door had read: "Gopal Sharma-Astrologer " and instantly the visitors knew that they were face to face with the astrologer himself. Gopal was expecting them as per their tele request of last night and ushered them in with folded hands as per tradition. They found themselves in a largish courtyard with a huge peepal tree in the Centre that appeared to be centuries old looking at the vast network of intricate branches. Parvati observed that it had been decorated with vermillion, which adorned holy, respected structures. The formal introductions over Gopal called for buttermilk made from cow milk and they settled for a tete that lasted for a couple of hours surprisingly. Gopal shared with them old family documents that established his ancestral links to Pandit Ved Vyas or Pandit Ji as Gopal lovingly called him. Once he clearly saw his visitors were convinced with his credentials, he spoke out humbly:

"Respected guests, may I now venture to inquire about the motive of your visit to my humble dwelling."

Dr Roy there upon shared the entire background with Gopal including the scroll and requested Him for help to unravel the missing Gita chapter. Gopal had been expecting them and once he knew that Dr. Roy was a neurologist everything his father had told him stood confirmed. A strange expression from Gopal greeted them as if he was lost in deep thoughts before he blurted out:

"Honoured visitors, what you have revealed corroborates what I have known. Yes, something very powerful is concealed on these premises since all our ancestors were told to expect the unraveling of a secret legacy of Pandit Ji in the age of Kalyuga. Come with me."

Gopal led them to the almirah in his father's room and opened it. The red cloth bound thin book containing the 19th chapter in the ancient dialect was then handed over to Dr. Roy. The photocopy of the same was e-mailed to the Lama for getting the translation done. This would save time.

That evening, Dr Roy together with Parvati invited Gopal to their hotel for an early dinner. Destiny has strange ways to honour itself as sometimes one meets one's destiny on the road one has taken to avoid it. Parvati knew that initially she was reluctant to accompany Adam to the Nobel event. Her doing so had kick started a chain of events that had led to her meeting first Dr Roy and now Gopal. Talking to him that evening made her feel she knew him for ages almost like a brother she never had. Gopal was an enigma. He had been taught astrology and the ancient scriptures at home while he graduated in the domain of Quantum physics. As he shared his life with both the others that evening two things mystically seemed to merge in his personality—the head and the heart. Rarely had Parvati seen intellectual brilliance combine so well with emotional depth in a single human. The rare specimen was before her now. Her thoughts were interrupted by Gopal's matter of fact voice stating that at times what Science was discovering today was already enunciated in the ancient scriptures. Dr Roy asked for an example. Gopal lit up as he said:

"Dr Roy, do you remember the law of conservation of matter taught to high school students of physics?...well in the Vedas the chanting of the popular verse in every Hindu home means exactly the same. It starts with the words: Purnamidam Purnamidah."

Dr Roy immediately recognized it as he had often chanted it at religious family functions without being aware of the meaning exactly.

That a modern vital scientific law was enunciated millennia ago in a scripture was amazing. He patted Gopal on the back for pointing out this awesome fact. It was getting late as the threesome finished dinner. As Gopal said goodbye Parvati impulsively spoke up:

"Dr. Roy...Could we request Gopal to accompany us to meet His Holiness when the secret translated Chapter 19 is read out."

7

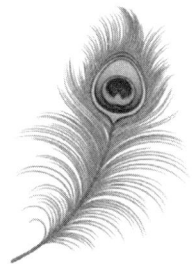

THE DIVINE VISION

Mcleodganj also known as 'Little Lhasa" lies on the foothills of the Himalayas near Dharamshala and is the capital of Tibet's Government in exile. Dr Roy and Parvati accompanied by Gopal landed at Dharamshala airport to proceed directly to meet his Holiness who had been duly informed and had arranged for the translator to be present when the trio from Kurukshetra arrived. As they alighted from the plane, Dr. Roy stumbled but Gopal was quick to hold him. A strange feeling came to the learned neurologist that a son like and daughter like companions were with him at this juncture of life. He was looking forward to meeting The Lama now.

His holiness welcomed them warmly and congratulated them on their historic discovery. An affectionate hug for Gopal from the Lama, and the meeting started as the translator entered the room that moment. Dr. Roy handed over the photographed copy of the entire Chapter 19. A scanned copy of Pandit ji's secret Chapter had preceded their visit and a translation in English had already been made by the learned translator, a middle aged Tibetan who had been living in London for a few years. The fresh herbal tea arrived in cream coloured China mugs with red dragons embossed on them. The Lama looked around and saw 6 anxious eyes riveted on the translator. An air of tense expectancy ruled as all present knew of the vital significance of what would be read out shortly. The secret chapter written millennia ago would rip open the present to usher a fantastic future for man, they knew.

The translator now proceeded to read out from a printed sheet of bond paper in chaste English. It ran thus:

On the battlefield of Kurukshetra where Krishna stood with his outstretched right palm blessing the kneeling Arjuna immediately after he had experienced the divine form of Krishna where the deity was shown as the infinite universe in eternity, an urgent query arose in the intellect of Arjuna on which he asked the following question of his mentor:

"Oh learned Krishna, please explain how I a mere mortal and a human with limited mental and conscious abilities was able to experience your infinite and eternal manifestation instantly...what power did you grant me and in what manner that I evolved so exponentially to be able to experience and be blessed by this divine vast vision just granted to me and denied to normal humans...I await your answer with bated breath My Lord..."

Krishna took a second before his thoughts took the shape of words of wisdom that would one day implode humanity

THE DIVINE VISION

into a neo-evolved race walking on the unique planet called Earth. The frozen moment of Arjuna kneeling in front of Krishna's blessed palm on the battleground of Kurukshetra would acquire a tumultuous echo forever in the History of Humanity after Krishna's answer to Arjuna which ran thus:

"My dearest Arjuna,

I salute you for this awesome intellectual question. Let me explain to you and through you to future human generations a divine vision of their coming ascent towards a stupendous evolution that awaits them. I did not grant you any extra powers to experience my divine form...this power is already inbuilt in you and in each human.

All I did was to awaken it. As I blessed you with my outstretched palm emanated powerful vibrations towards your kneeling forehead and as the catalyst like Ray's struck a particular point in your brain it unleashed your own potential to spiritually evolve and comprehend my vision by actually experiencing it.

What I activated today will be self-activated by the human race at the end of Kaliyuga age...The skills will come from a man of brain science and lead to an amazing ascent for man on his journey of a conscious evolution...Through my answer to you, oh Arjuna, I hereby point out the direction to future man but the path has to be walked by them themselves. The human brain as the future sciences will reveal one day is divided into two parts, one intuitive and the other analytic. This division prevents a holistic vision for the human race. However there is a unique single meeting point between the two brain hemi-spheres that apparently divides the two parts but is in fact meant to unify them. The techniques will come through the brain science of that age...Of course I shall be there too as per my promise to humanity that whenever evil rears its head My Avatar will come to make good forces win...This final time my 10th Avatar will not only help good to triumph over evil but also evolve humanity to a higher dimension for all times."

Arjuna was dumbstruck by Krishna's answer as his mentor approached him and asked him to rise from the battleground where he was still kneeling and reeling due to the unprecedented experience of that day. As Krishna hugged Arjuna he whispered in his ear:

"Relax Arjuna, I shall be there too in Kalyuga..."

The Translator stopped reading as Chapter 19 of the Gita had ended.

There was pin drop silence in the room but Dr Roy could hear his own thoughts clearly which ran thus:

"My God, this centuries old scripture is indicating the exact structure of the human mind including the specific point dividing the two brain hemispheres that neurology discovered much later. How?"

Dr. Roy knew now the exact brain point Krishna was referring to as the possible unifying point of the brain. Modern neurology has given it a name. It was called The Pineal Gland.

As the translator stopped reading the secret "Chapter 19" of the Gita in English, there was silence in the room for a few seconds. Each one was in his or her own way absorbing

THE DIVINE VISION

the implications of a revelation that was truly majestic in its vision. The words of Krishna as written by Ved Vyasa was a mighty reassurance to mankind about an awesome transcendence for humanity. The time had come. The chapter kept under wraps for centuries must be revealed. The amazing part was the promise made by Krishna on the battlefield of Kurukshetra to Arjuna that 'I will be there'. Each one present in the room with His Holiness believed in the promise and was pondering over this same point. Where was Krishna now?

It was the Lama who broke the silence that held a vibrant potential potency of sorts.

The reading of the translated secret chapter 19 of the Gita,, in the presence of The Lama was a deep experience for Parvati, Gopal and Dr Roy himself. It was as if a foggy veil of ignorance had been suddenly lifted from the Nobel neurologist's mind and a narrow but clear-cut pathway lay in front of him. Dr. Roy's brain was working fast as if on auto mode. The fact that the secret chapter was concerned with brain sciences and he happened to be the top human in the field now made him shudder. A vast vision was being offered to him to serve and uplift humanity.

The path had been shown to him. He had to now walk on it to reach the destination. As the Lama spoke up all ears were listening with rapt attention.

"Interesting...deeply interesting...Did all of you notice the reference to brain science in this secret revelatory chapter...and just see the coincidence that the most learned man of brain science is the first to be revealed this hitherto hidden chapter of the Gita...I see a powerful cosmic intelligence at work here...what say you..."

The lama was looking directly at Dr Roy now who was vigorously nodding in agreement. Gopal spoke up:

"This is a cosmic destiny at work...it is strange but I know for a fact now through my experience that a powerful force is constantly at work in guiding human affairs. One can call it destiny maybe but it is an intelligent force and not to be ignored. As an astrologer I have closely witnessed it in the affairs of individuals but here I see it moving or rather pushing the human race towards the destined future...the ascent of man to maybe a higher stage of evolution as the scripture reveals..."

Parvati cleared her throat and added:

"One perception seems very clear to me...we have to take the baton forward from here...the scripture is giving us a vibrant push to probe in a particular direction for human advancement and it is up to those present here to undertake this quest as a team I feel with a leader well suited and qualified for the mission...and we all know who that leader is..."

Another phase of absolute silence followed, a kind of emptiness or 'Shunyata' as the Lama would put it that had the full power of potential that would in turn provide the tremendous energy to unfold a divine vision for man.

All eyes were on Dr. Roy now including those of The Lama who spoke up confidently:

"Are you ready for Krishna's challenge, Doctor ?"

In the same second, Laik was at the Lama's feet and as the spiritual leader hugged the future Team leader who had now agreed to take up the quest, there were tears in all eyes.

The sacred journey towards mankind's higher evolution had started.

It was most intriguing that a learned man of science was conducting a vital research on a clue provided by a historic description of the only written recorded instance in the history of man of a human brain being able to experience an infinite phenomenon namely Arjuna's vision of Krishna's infinite being on the battlefield of Kurukshetra.

As The Begum was landing at Dubai International Airport, her daughter Parvati was just leaving from the Lama's personal headquarters along with Dr. Roy and Gopal to hold a meeting among themselves at their hotel room to chart out the future course of action. The mission that destiny had handed down to them was now proactive. The ambience at Dharamshala was festive as the Tibetan festival of Losar was on.

It was a bizarre set of circumstances that had got three individuals together joined by a common bond. Dr Roy had lately been feeling that he had acquired something that he had always missed and that was a family. Parvati and Gopal were like a son and daughter to him and they too felt a father figure in him. The crux of the issue was research to be conducted on the lines of the clues given by the revelation of the secret Gita chapter. Dr. Roy was inspired and wanted to tie up with The Brain Institute at New York, which was doing pioneering research on the unknown frontiers of the brain and human consciousness itself. Parvati it was decided would handle the media part from time to time and Gopal had sincerely offered to act as Dr. Roy's personal assistant and travel with him including to New York if necessary. As these thoughts were being aired, Parvati's cell jingled. It was Adam.

"Where are you darling...missing u...Also you are required here professionally..."

Parvati discreetly answered:

"Missing you too darling. Shall be reaching Dubai by tomorrow. See you soon..."

She cut short the conversation to listen to the Doctor's concluding remarks:

"Gopal, let us contact the New York Brain Institute and ask for a month's research association with Dr. Brauner the head of the Institute and accordingly get our tickets done...Yes you are appointed as my personal assistant from this moment onwards and yes, I am starting a new Foundation with the Nobel prize money and you would be the executive Director with financial and other allied powers. As for you Parvati, we will bother you as and when required and I will be requesting Adam to spare you for a few days shortly to visit us at New York and see how our research shapes up. Parvati, your role as a media historian is going to be vital..."

The learned Professor knew that the tie up with the New

York Institute would give acceleration to their journey to activate the Gita plan. He had already introduced himself and his work to the Board members of the Institute and they were very impressed. All that was required was to go to see at first hand what specific experiments were being conducted and soon the stage would be set for a quantum leap towards the goals so dear to the Lama.

The thought that struck all of them was that temporarily they would be parting only to reunite soon. The anniversary of the ghastly 9/11 event at the twin towers was coming up in due course and Dr Roy wanted that all three attend it. It had been the most gruesome act of terror in contemporary times and Parvati could find a historic event that somewhat matched the cruelty of this horror.

The crucifixion of Christ.

Gopal was amazed how he had been gripped in a bizarre quest involving a subject he had scant knowledge about. He had heard of the Brain Institute of New York and vaguely recalled how their research had led to some innovative theories about the human mind and its potentiality but the fact that he would one day be intimately tied up with the Institute one day was amazing.

This now was a diabolic destiny at work moving slowly at times and flowing like a torrent at others. They were in the same boat now and it was to be seen what the future held in store for them. As they said their goodbyes three pairs of eyes were moist simultaneously. Emotional unity had been struck here and now.

8

EMOTIONAL BONDS

Adam was looking forward to Parvati's arrival in Dubai that evening. The flight was delayed and he had instructed his chauffeur to drive her straight to his home. To their home. Soon they would be wed. The forces of physical attraction when combined with an emotive bond resulted in a powerful concoction called love. It is such a state of being that uplifts the human experience to new levels of peace and joy and this anticipatory feeling was dawning on Adam. In what seemed to be a crazy fit he had decorated his entire apartment with red roses. Soon she would be here in his arms and they would be chatting away the whole night. That moment the bell jingled and she walked looking as sweet and beautiful as could be in the side slit red dress. He embraced her tightly and both were lost in a timeless symphony without a name. When they emerged from their trance it was dawn.

A stage comes rarely when one can create an alternate life for oneself and Parvati had successfully reached that level. She could never believe that the day that she had dreamed about had finally arrived. This was it. A companion for life ,hopefully, who was intelligent, handsome and reformed meant a lot and to share goals in life meant a tremendous lot indeed. In the evening she would be welcoming her mother ,Begum Bano ,who would have reached back from India. Although Begum knew Adam it would be the first time they would be meeting in the capacity of a different relation. Parvati looked forward to the private dinner that night where all three would meet.

The day went by quickly at the Burj Khalifa office with Parvati getting a new important assignment to cover a memorial service at the Twin towers to be attended by The American President.

She welcomed the assignment, as Dr. Roy and Gopal would be there too in connection with their brain research.. The evening came after what seemed a long wait but promised to be a good gain. The Begum was delighted to meet Adam and as they gently hugged the senior lady blessed him. At that moment a stronger bond was being formed between them. It was there already and they had worked together as representatives of the media and diplomatic worlds for human benefit as they did about the Russian-American summit but now it was purely personal with Parvati acting as a strong bond. The soup arrived and the talk subsided. Begum felt joy after a long time tingling into her as she saw them together. She knew the inner core of both well enough to understand their different worlds that somehow would develop meeting points as time elapsed. Opposites attract and sometimes fatally so but not this time. They would be OK together barring the occasional fireworks, Bano somehow knew. She missed Parvati's father whom nature had snatched away at a young age. It was destiny that had propelled the Begum to become a professional diplomat and lead her to be where she was now.

The dinner arrived and the chit chat started. Parvati updated them about her recent experiences with Dr. Roy, The Lama, Gopal and how the research on brain evolution would be continued at New York. Adam mentioned that Parvati was to go to interview a very important person in New York soon and would have occasion to meet them there. The Begum asked the identity of the important interviewee. Adam commented that it was the Director of the CIA.

It is said that wisdom does not remove sorrow but only gives strength to bear it. That night, the Begum was in a nostalgic mood. Nature had been cruel to her when her life partner departed early leaving her alone to bring up a beautiful daughter, the symbol of their love. Today that daughter was all set to proceed on her own life journey and nature had compensated them somewhat by sending Adam into their lives. The future was promising and soon the scars of yester years would go away. At that moment, the Begum noticed something moist trickling down her left cheek.

It was a solitary crystal clear droplet that had a special name.

A tear.

9

THE SENSUOUS WORLD

The aroma of olive oil intruding into the heated and moist concoction of chopped mushrooms, tomatoes and cheese reminded him simultaneously of Spain, Italy and the Mediterranean with Britain thrown in just as the exotic veggies were laid to rest on the double delectable omelette base. Adam's tongue was relishing the euro breakfast even as his eyes were inhaling pleasure surveying the female contours of the sensuous cook somewhat heightened by the manner she adorned the black and white apron apparel exclusively meant for the marble dominated kitchen. Parvati looked stunning in her velvet black lingerie partly peeping out from the short apron. He was relishing her and the dish and she was captivated by his hooked on expressions, especially his deep dumbo eyes. Ever since their Stockholm engagement their relationship had progressed steadily to what was popularly referred to as a 'live in' of course with the tacit approval of the Begum.

Adam's early breakfast was signed off with black coffee and cream and would be as usual followed by the Sunday shower and games in the Italian Jacuzzi. In one coordinated move he untied her apron and gently led her below the bathing section in the pure white tiled washroom dominated by long mirrors and natural sunlight. The pure Aqua ovals from the showers refreshed them together lost in the wanderlust of fabulous fantasies stimulated by the nudity reflected in the mirrors and distinctly delicious for the daring duo even as they merged into a locked embrace under the twin shower drops titillating their sensitive veins of pleasure spots galloping to a near simultaneous climax that left them miraculously moaning but still alive after the hectic bathing work out.

A rather busy day awaited Adam with business meetings scheduled throughout the day including those with bankers, stockholders and the works. However it was the final secret meeting that had not been even listed in his official engagements that he was looking forward to. An anonymous caller had contacted him for a 15 minute meeting at a somewhat secluded venue on the Dubai-Sharjah border. Normally Adam would have banged shut such a call but the caller's one sentence revelation made the vital difference between a yes and a No. The sentence was:

"Mr. Adam I know who murdered your former head of the Cellular Technology Division and Why."

Adam had been instantly jolted back to events some months back when he had appointed a bright young French technocrat Francis to that post. The alleged suicide of Francis ,within months of taking over, had sent shock ripples in the corporate world especially Adam who had developed affection and respect for the Frenchman. The police had closed the case as one of suicide by hanging on the basis of an alleged suicide note mentioning personal reasons for the suicide. Adam had been puzzled in the light of the last conversation with Francis who had gleefully informed him of an impending breakthrough. Till today, a sense of closure had eluded Adam in the matter. Even as Adam was battling with his office engagements, Parvati was in a relaxed mood after the succulent shower session. A short siesta and she started to put her wardrobe in order. The exercise took more than an hour with the only small locker remaining. As she groped to take the jewellery out it fell.

Her small black personal diary.

Special secret moments she had valued in her life were recorded here. She was in a dazed stupor as she started to flip through the pages while furtively glancing and almost fearfully glancing and almost withdrawing at times hesitant to go on but unable to stop. Alas a part of one's life cannot be chopped off. The flipping had stopped as her mascara laden eyes became moist, They were staring at a name in the diary:

'Shlaka...'

It was at Kent University while doing her media graduation that Parvati had met Shlaka the beautiful blonde from Athens who was her room-mate. Both were fatherless and were going through a lonely patch. A close friendship led to a more than closer bonding bordering on the physical though of course very briefly as they evolved confidence to go their separate ways. Parvati was lost in the deep eyes of the pic stapled to her diary when the phone rang. It was Adam:

"Hi Love...something urgent has come up...meet me at Sahara mall food court at 6 P.M. today...do not approach me but film me and the person I will be meeting there..."bye..."

The mobile clicked shut. Parvati still had the diary and picture in her hand. Slowly she proceeded to shred and tear the diary page and pic into small pieces and flush it down in the toilet. What was so dear to her once was sucked into oblivion now.

The British Broadcasting Corporation or the BBC, as it was popularly called, was to announce 'The Global News Director Award' and Parvati was being touted as the favourite nominee. The final announcement would be made at a glittering ceremony at Hotel Savoy. The Begum had been persuaded by her dear daughter to accompany her to London since Adam would be away to Tokyo on business.

London had always held a special charm for Parvati since she had graduated from the UK and had often visited London during vacations. She recalled her shopping sprees across Oxford street from Marble Arch to Tottenham Court end as well as Harrodsburg. The first day of their stay was rather

THE SENSUOUS WORLD 59

hectic with many shopping bags collected including dresses, purses and the likes. The Begum too indulged herself. Exhausted, they retired to bed early. That night Parvati had a pleasant dream. It was the night that she and Shalaka had travelled to London on a weekend and had to share a bed in London in a Soho Hotel. The tossing and turning on the narrow bed was a wee uncomfortable but not without a shade of forbidden momentary pleasure soon to become a relic of history.

The next morning the glittering gala dinner was being awaited eagerly in Global media circles. Who would be the winner. The Begum was sure her daughter deserved it. Parvati's documentary on the dangers of human extinction caused by atomic conflict would win the day. The gong sounded and the Director of the BBC announced there had been a tie for first place. As the first name was announced The Begum was ecstatic. Parvati proudly walked up the stage to receive The Golden Pen just as her co-winner walked up too. Utter amazement arrested Parvati as she looked up to see her co-winner. It was none other than Shalaka.

The formalities over they all settled down to a delicious round table dinner as both friends chatted of days gone by. The Begum wanted to know more about Shalaka's documentary 'Inside China'. The name of Madame Lee who Shalaka had interviewed cropped up. Shalaka remarked that her impression was that Madame Lee was close to the Chairman. There the meet ended as Shalaka's husband was waiting outside. The Emirates flight landed on time smoothly and as they passed the green channels they knew a new future awaited them. A daughter who was returning home with global accolades and looking ahead of a joyous life with a near perfect partner that destiny had delivered at her doorstep. A mother whose sole aim in life was to ensure peace and development on the globe.

How far each one would be able to fructify their life vision only time would tell.

10

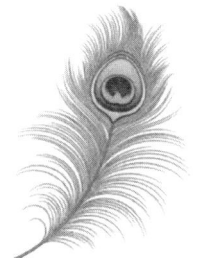

A Tryst with Terror

New York was now a concrete jungle minus the massive twin towers of 9/11 fame.10 million sq. ft. of office space standing more than 1300 ft. high each tower weighing 2,50,000 tons was no more than a memorial now with water flowing into the nothingness of 2 huge square black holes with the names of the 2983 victims inscribed along the parapets. Parvati's first emotion on seeing the memorial could best be described as seismic.

It was in this public rendezvous that she was slated to meet the Director of the CIA, away from the gaze of his office staff. Adam had meticulously set up the clandestine encounter as requested by his friend the Director whom he loved to address as Tiger since his full formal name Roberto Jefferson Patton was rather longish. Tiger was a very close confidant of the President having been personal friends earlier. The relationship had withstood the test of time thanks to the respect each had for the abilities of the other. An urgent request from Tiger for an immediate personal meet up with

Adam's confidante had Parvati board the direct Emirates flight to New York from Dubai a day earlier and now she stood at the appointed spot at the appointed time waiting to be approached. No other details had been specified.

The flowing water was disappearing into the huge square holes where once stood the majestic twin towers and the accompanying almost musical flowing ripples transported Parvati momentarily into a higher dimension where her individuality seemed to merge in the poignant aura of the powerful ground on which so many had faced a violent exit from this world thanks to terrorism. So engrossed was she, oblivious of the breeze playing with her blonde hair, that she hardly noticed a tall and lanky middle aged man with a bowler hat, an overcoat and rust shades standing right next to her.

A forced cough made her land back to reality and as she looked back as he extended his hand and whispered:

"Tiger"

They shook hands as he motioned to her to walk around the memorial. It was early morning and there was hardly anyone around as they paced around for the crucial informal chat that day. The formal interview would follow tomorrow at the Director's office in full gaze of the world media. Roberto impressed Parvati by his clear and concise conversation even as she was mentally absorbing all he was revealing. His words were subdued but clearly audible as he spoke authoritatively:

"Madam, Please convey my gratitude to Adam for this quickly organized meeting. Speed is vital in intelligence matters and more so in matters concerning China. It has been some time now that we have been observing a specific area under Chinese occupation through satellite imagery which has its limitations but one thing is very clear. The Chinese army is on the verge of a breakthrough and our agents within the people's republic assure us that the impending breakthrough is in the development of an extremely deadly new variant of The Atomic Bomb 100 fold more powerful and virulent than that known to mankind till date. It involves the discovery of a neo-nuclear substance that is being harvested with evil destructive intentions to ensure Chinese hegemony. Our drones have identified the hub where this demonic activity is being carried out but we are unable to infiltrate further inside. However, a lucky opportunity has suddenly cropped up."

The Director paused here to look around. Surreptitious surveillance was called to foresee any dangerous situation. His mind was activated now as he welcomed this lady's visit to interview him.

Global media had clout and the exposure would do his image good looking to his secret ambition to shortly run for the presidency. He lit his cigar and continued:

"The Chinese premier has in a false pretense announced that they would open up parts of this very location where we suspect clandestine activity is on. These particular coordinates also happen to be held as very sacred by a large segment of Indians. The Chinese have also allowed media representatives as part of the pilgrimage so that China is able to establish its good credentials with neighboring nations. I want Adam's media team to go inside and gather crucial evidence of what the Chinese are up to..."

His voice trailed as Parvati spoke up even as understanding dawned upon her:

"Sir, which is this powerful holy spot in China that you are referring to..."

The answer was like a bullet shot:

"Mount Kailash, the abode of Shiva, in Chinese occupied Tibet."

The CIA headquarters was a power Centre secured to the hilt especially the section occupied by the Director. Parvati of course had the necessary clearances to interview the chief or 'Tiger' as Adam would have addressed him. There were only a handful of trusted aides along with the cameraman at the time of the brief bites given to Global Media Inc. by the head of the most powerful security agency in the world. Only a day earlier the President's press secretary in a White House briefing had revealed the contents of the President's friendly message to the Chairman of the People's Republic of China. The world media had been commenting on the very soft tone and almost subjugating content of the President's overture to Beijing in sharp contrast to the normally tough stance taken by earlier Presidents against China. The purpose of The Director in giving the interview to a friendly channel, that would be visible around the globe, soon became clear to Parvati as she asked the vital question as directed by Adam. She cleared her throat and in a matter of fact tone asked The Director:

"Sir, In the context of the contemporary global scenario, as head of the CIA, what are your views on China."

The camera was focused on Tiger's stern face as he responded:

"Parvati, thanks for asking this question. I want to put on record that the United States of America has always pursued a policy of peace and friendship with all nations but let it be clear to all that we will not tolerate any action by China that has evil intent to impose its hegemony on global affairs. Period."

That moment the tidal thought hit her. Parvati grasped it in a second. Adam's powerful channel was being used by Tiger to launch his own Presidential candidature in the coming American elections. Henceforth the world would see him as a tough guy in the role of the next President of the US of A, as compared to the dovish and weak present incumbent. The Director had well accomplished his goal as Parvati could gather from his smug smile and warm handshake at the end of the interview.

Parvati had completed her professional assignment with The Director of the CIA and it was around noon. Time for personal affairs now. She was looking forward with her lunch tete-a-tete with Gopal who was already in New York with Dr. Roy as part of the Lama's initiative to put them in touch with the American neurologists research team probing on the potential of the human brain. She had taken a cab till Broadway and alighted near McDonalds where she now awaited Gopal.

He was on time as he joined her on the corner table she had selected. It was a pleasant hour for both as they updated each other since their last meeting. Then something astounding happened that left both of them happily jolted. They saw Dr. Roy approaching. He could not resist the joy of being with them and had slipped away from the lab that had been his second home for the last few days. That pleasant day, he had not gone to his computerized lab but had preferred McDonalds. Google he now knew could answer most questions...for others he would need meditation and research.

As he approached Gopal and Parvati, there was a childlike glee in the core of his heart.

Dr. Roy was loving this moment with two youngsters who had become almost a part of his being, strange as it may sound.

Hugs followed by a cafe latte led to an interesting analysis of Parvati's meeting with the CIA Director with Dr. Roy making the suggestion that Parvati should take Gopal along with her to Mt. Kailash as an escort. In the meantime The Professor would complete his neurological research in conjunction with his American associates as per The Lama's wishes, which was proving very productive till now. There was an air of childish excitement in Roy's voice as he exclaimed:

"My children. I am sure I am permitted to call both of you that. I am so positive of a breakthrough in my research shortly. Things are hotting up."

The youngsters nodded in approval. Parvati could sense a kindly childishness in the eminent neurologist before interjecting:

It was Gopal's turn to add:

"Indeed it is my humble privilege to be a small part of this awesome process that might well help elevate human consciousness to the highest dimension."

The aromatic coffee was stimulating the threesome towards a strange unity in an unnamed quest that they somehow knew would prove vital to man one day. What they did not know was the looming imminent and pulsating danger that would soon appear as an evil obstacle to their personal security and their global goal...

The Global Media Inc. carried the interview of the Director of CIA at prime time the same day as instructed by Adam. The interview caused uproar as during the interview the Director made a statement that did not seem to be in unison with the President's stand taken a day earlier. One fact became apparent. 'Tiger' had proved worth his nickname and was now very much in the Presidential race of America.

As he watched the interview from his Dubai head office, Adam besides admiring Parvati's cheek bones felt satisfied in a job well done that would maybe help to establish a dear friend at the helm of affairs in the most powerful house on the globe—The White House. Adam was glad he had sent Parvati to America for this interview. He knew her abilities to draw out the interviewee out of his shell by her put on coquettish tactics although he knew that her core was purity personified. As a result of the telecast, the popularity ratings of Adam's channel shot up substantially. Adam now eagerly looked forward to a life with a dear partner both personally and professionally.

Gopal had a restless night as he tossed and turned thinking about the intuitive dream he had had earlier that night after which he had not been able to sleep. It was about his ancestral home that he had dreamt about where the secret chapter of the Gita had been found. It was amazing how life had moved swiftly for him recently and how new people had come to play a significant role in his life. The dream had a subconscious message for him he believed recollecting the details of the dream in which the ancient tree is splitting into two as lightning strikes his home and the secret chapter is about to be destroyed but he saves it in time.

When someone sees doom approaching, the first reaction is to prepare for the coming ordeal. Gopal is lost but decides to go along with Parvati to China. The twin towers attack had happened on 9/11 and ever since then terrorism had taken a new form.

A new virulent form, more virulent, more deadly than ever before. Gopal's astrological calculations revealed that soon the next deadly terror event would occur. Intuitively, he knew he would be at the event place then. He just knew it. It was the mighty force called Destiny at work...silently, stealthily, and mercilessly. He as an astrologer was a trader of this power and all too familiar with its working. In moments of heightened awareness he had experienced strange cosmic insights that had seemed to empower him tremendously about individual and global destinies and their eerie overlapping. Sometimes the omens took the shape of dreams and slowly the dark veil of ignorance seemed to be lifting followed by flashes of brilliant light. This was one such phase now.

And then it all became crystal clear.

He recalled an entire night in his teens when his grandfather had lectured and explained to him how the wheel of destiny worked. It was all a network. Individual roles were interlinked and ultimately connected to global events. The future was just an unfolding of the present based upon the past happening on the fabric of physical existence and happening continuously. As a student of Science, Gopal had listened intently to his grandfather and one phrase of Einstein had popped up in his mind then : 'The Space-time Continuum.'

There was a link, call it Karmic, between his meeting Parvati and Dr Roy and the subsequent revelation granted to him of the secret Gita chapter and his visit to N York and now to China. His individual destiny had now been interlinked with that of Dr Roy and Parvati and all their individual destinies had been hooked up to global phenomena namely the activation of the secret chapter of the Gita to mankind. Human destiny was making him a wheel to move on or so it seemed. He had to move with the flow. No turning back. His rich heritage had got him to the crossroads. Now he must march forward.

The mobile whistled and he was instantly up. It was Dr. Roy wishing him bon-voyage for his journey to Mt. Kailash along with Parvati that morning. It had all been arranged by Adam. They would be the first batch to visit Mt Kailash after it was temporarily opened by the Chinese. Dr Roy told him that he would complete his research in America and then go to The Lama at Mcleodganj and Gopal should join him there along with Parvati on his return from Mt. Kailash. Gopal could clearly sense the mighty force pushing him and the others in a particular direction.

Hardly had Dr Roy put down the phone, Parvati rang up Gopal.

There was news. Parvati's mom had conveyed to Adam who had in turn called her up to share that an anonymous mail had been received by the Begum from someone powerful inside China. The mail was encrypted and could not be re-traced. It read as follows:

"I am known to you Begum Bano and I will reveal my identity at the right time. My country has turned evil and is plotting against the globe...shall reveal details shortly..."

11

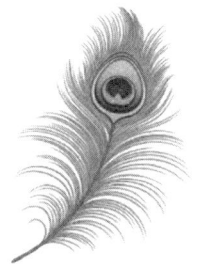

THE EVIL ENCOUNTER

Adam was staring in amazement at Begum Bano as they surveyed the vast Dubai horizon from atop Burj Khalifa. He had only one question in his mind. Who the hell was the anonymous Emailer. The Begum had no answers but yes there was one clue and a vital one at that. The mailer had to be someone high up in the Chinese hierarchy and someone who somehow knew the Begum a little It was a most interesting day in the city of lights as Dubai was often called. The duo was admiring the lights from the top of The Burj. Adam said he had had a talk with the CIA Director and informed him about his team's visit to Mt Kailash to coordinate their surveillance and security. The Director had assured him of the needful back up to ensure the safety of Parvati and Gopal. The US satellite services would be working to assist Adam's team, Patton had assured Adam while thanking him for the terrific exposure world wide of The interview. The President had reprimanded Tiger and left it at that but Patton's star was shining now much above the political horizon.

The Begum was still apprehensive. What if the safety of her daughter was compromised? Adam at the behest of the Director wanted his team to try and infiltrate beyond the tourist area deeper into the clandestine nuclear activity inside Mt Kailash as indicated by the American Satellite images. It was imperative that the security of the news team was not compromised. Only a day remained for their flight to China. Adam had briefed Parvati on the basis of inputs from the CIA regarding clandestine activity around the Mansarover lake near the Mt. Kailash.

The gesture of the Chinese authorities to open up the holy precincts to visitors coincided with the Hindu festival of 'Shivaratri' dedicated to Lord Shiva whose abode was supposed to be Mt. Kailash mythologically. This was a diplomatic move to show the friendship and tolerance of the Chinese regime towards other religions. In reality, it was a bluff to camouflage the hegemonic aspirations of The Chairman of The People's Republic of China.

It was decided that Adam would keep Begum informed and that satisfied her to some extent besides Patton's reassurances but then she was a mom. They together had a good working relationship which would now be converted into a personal one with Parvati and Adam tying the knot. Suddenly Adam asks: "Dinner"

The Begum agrees. They walk down to The Armani Hotel for a typical Indian cuisine of Tandoori chicken and black lentils with butter Naan. They are after all both from the

THE EVIL ENCOUNTER

Indian subcontinent. The food was immaculate and the talk minimal with only a climax on the matter of the timing of Parvati's marriage. Adam wanted an early marriage but Begum wanted time. The matter was left to be decided by Parvati. Her choice would prevail. There the matter rested. It is rare that a tripartite link lasts but this one would. As the Begum got up to go she gave an affectionate hug to Adam. It was for the first time that he addressed her as Mom.

The Begum had a tense night thinking about Parvati in China. As sleep overtook her, she was in a different nightmarish world. A dull throbbing permeated through her numb skull leaving the world spinning with a constant nauseous thudding at the back of her head that was overpowering all thought and reason. The dawn chorus seemed warbled with the dew on the daisies glimmering in the first rays of sunlight. The leaves fluttered delicately in the aromatic breeze. Beads of water glittered at the tips of her hazel eyes streaming down her once care-free face depicting the anguish she felt that echoed across the forlorn cavern that was Begum's fragmented heart.

It was a hand, a pale human hand drained of life, wilted and frail. Parvati was in danger, blood was gushing out of her daughter's head, draining out the arteries. A musty odour meandered in the Begum's nostrils.. Suddenly a sharp pulsating alarm from the Begum's ornate mobile pierced her interiors to wake her up with a jolt. The nightmare had ended.

Parvati and Gopal were on time to catch the flight to

Beijing and there they would have to register with the authorities before proceeding to Mt. Kailash. It had been reassuring to hear from Adam that the Director CIA had assured him that their team would be watched over by the US agencies. Anyways, as a journalist she was bold but always cautious. It was Gopal she was a bit anxious for. Lately she had been treating him as a kid brother of sorts. Gopal had laughed off any mention of dangers and was viewing it more like an adventure of sorts. Together, they would have to somehow infiltrate behind apparent scenarios to get to the core of the problem. Adam had briefed her well.

The journey by bus was arduous and tiring and involved mountain terrain. There were other journalists/photographers besides pilgrims from different nations that had come to see Mt. Kailash and the Chinese authorities were keeping a close vigil. There would be an overnight stay and the back journey would commence the next evening. By the time they reached the base of Mt. Kailash, it was dusk and in another half hour it would be dark. They checked into their allotted tent. In the dim light Parvati could see Lake Mansarovar a little distance away. She was instantly alerted as per Adam's info that this was the area of the clandestine activity. In the morning they would be moving ahead to visit the holy temple of Shiva at the first ridge atop Mt. Kailash. Only the night remained for Gopal and her to do their snooping assignment. She whispered this update to Gopal as they entered their tent under the gaze of the Chinese militia who were constantly supervising the whole batch of visitors.

It was around mid-night that their sleep was disrupted due to a continuous medium drilling sound. Parvati woke up Gopal and together they exited the tent to witness a bizarre view. Against the darkish horizon Parvati could see a convoy of military trucks being hurtled across into a side lane entering the mountain. Gopal saw strange electromagnetic gadgets vanishing into the cave entrance to the mountain. Surreptitiously Gopal and Parvati set off towards the cave and were lucky to enter inside by riding on the boot extension of a jeep.

Inside they saw a bizarre clearing with scores of vehicles parked randomly. It was apparent that some sort of drilling/mining activity was being conducted and pieces of a somewhat fluorescent rock were being cut out from the mountain side. Parvati saw the staff wearing visors of the sort worn when dealing with radioactive substances. Gopal nodded when she mentioned it. A guard's cough alerted them and they made a quick escape back to their tent. The next morning the pilgrims were taken around the Shiva temple formally in full view of the world media. China had scored a point that it was a free nation encouraging all religions to prosper simultaneously.

Gopal and Parvati now knew that Mt Kailash had become a source of radioactive material that would be presumably used by the Chinese in a neo form of Nuclear bomb technology. An hour later the Director had before him Adam's report on his team's surveillance. They had unearthed info that satellite imagery had failed to do. It was a vital lead and

The Director personally called up and thanked Adam and assured him that America would take the necessary steps to safeguard the globe against Chinese evil designs.

Adam was now waiting for Parvati's return. Gopal would be rejoining Dr Roy for a few days in the USA as per a modified plan. Begum Bano was feeling restless and missing her daughter. Soon they would all be reunited in Dubai.

12

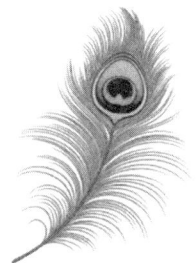

THE BREAKTHROUGH

It is said that knowledge can be communicated but not wisdom. Dr Roy sought both. The quest to empower the human brain to attain the vision of Chapter 19 of the Gita was no joke and he knew.

The American Centre for brain research set up by Dr. Brauner had all the facilities and infrastructure to facilitate Dr Roy's sojourn. The Lama had guided them well. Along with Gopal a detailed timetable had been prepared for research and observations of 20 meditating monks in the hope of a breakthrough. Most scientific inquiry is meticulous and thrives on the capability of the basic instrument of observation and analysis namely the brain. The awesome part now was that the subject of inquiry was this very instrument namely the brain. This observation and research was turning more and more away from the objective to the subjective dimensions. Gopal's study of astrological indications had already clearly indicated a partial breakthrough shortly in New York followed by a complete one, later at Mcleodganj the headquarters of the Lama.

The learned neurologist had delved into observation of various clinical aspects of meditative practices and interpolated them with quantum mechanics and neuro sciences but to no avail. It was a bright Sunday in New York and the lab was closed. Gopal and Dr. Roy were having a stroll in the Central Park and Gopal happened to mention a query raised in the ancient Vedas.

The central park was an urban park in Manhattan located between 5th avenue in the east and eight avenue in the west and was the most visited park in the United States. It was the pond at the park's south east corner that presented a beautiful spectacle to the walking visitor and it was as Dr. Roy and Gopal strolled on the pathway marking the periphery of the pond that Gopal was mentioning the Vedic thought that was in turn to kick start the neurologist's neurons towards a neo thinking pattern. The lush greenery surrounded by skyscrapers on the horizon landscape provided a peaceful island in the ocean of tumultuous turmoil of the concrete jungle in the city of New York. It was no doubt a popular haunt for visitors numbering above 35 million annually, who indulged in events like concerts, tours, sports, yoga and the jogging besides just plain strolling as the Indians duo were engaged at the very moment.

A very small step ahead sometimes helps to put things in perspective. Dr Roy had been grappling with a strange conundrum since the last few days at the meditation sessions at New York. The EEG readings of meditating Buddhist monks were revealing new patterns suggesting the expansion of human awareness to unprecedented levels but the final frontiers were still to be attained.

The barrier to experience infinity by a finite brain entity seemed impossible. It was in the Central Park that the cryptic comment by Gopal set the learned Neurologist thinking. Gopal was relating a Vedic query where an ancient text poses the question:

'What is the difference between space inside an earthen empty pot and the space outside it that engulfs and surrounds it?'

Gopal was commenting as he was casually strolling keeping Dr Roy's pace and emphatically stated that actually the distinction was arbitrary and in fact there was no distinction between the two spaces both of which formed parts of the same infinite entity called space.

Dr. Roy's penetrative mode of thinking had by now been fully activated. He knew that the individual limited entity could not experience its basic infinite nature by trying to let the infinite enter it. That would be unattainable. What it could do so was to remove the arbitrary distinction and merge with or penetrate into the infinite and let the infinite experience linger. A finite entity could not possibly accommodate an infinite entity but it could enter and merge into the infinite entity. That was the only way. Dr Roy was aware of bounded human consciousness as well as the infinite singularity consciousness. The neurological pathway from the former to the latter would involve two steps namely dissolution of the individual pineal gland to unify and empower the human brain consciousness and the subsequent ascent into the infinite consciousness. The second step needed a link up.

Dr. Roy's knowledge and wisdom were racing to trace this link up as he stared at the blank computer screen in front of him. Eureka. The Nobel laureate hit upon the link in a flash. The open ended dendrites embedded in the human brain which seemed to be purposeless a second ago now loomed large on the screen. This was the link and only channel for the human brain to merge and experience the infinite.

This was what Krishna had empowered Arjuna to 'see' Krishna's true infinite being. How Dr Roy would achieve this was an awesome puzzle that seemed to taunt the neurologist that very micro moment.

The flight back from China to Dubai gave Parvati an opportunity to make up her sleep. Sleep was like a balm for tired minds.

Adam had been in constant touch with her and she looked forward to spending time with him as well as her mom now in Dubai. The crucial purpose of the Mt Kailash sojourn had been so successful in so much that the Director CIA now knew what he was up against and would accordingly take steps to defeat the "dragon's" moves.

Adam welcomed her with a tight hug and they had a short siesta till the musical jingle of Parvati's mobile woke them up. It was her mom calling them over for dinner at her place. They accepted gladly. There were still a few hours to

THE BREAKTHROUGH

go before the evening invite and Adam wanted to discuss future personal plans with Parvati. He held her hand and wanted to know her views on the timing of their marriage. A moments silence and then she blurted out:

"Adam, nothing will be happening till Dr. Roy, Gopal and I reach somewhere on the Gita mission. I hope you will understand..."

Adam kissed her and nodded and there the matter would rest.

Begum Bano was looking forward to the evening but subconsciously another matter was on her mind. The G8 conference was coming up in Paris and all top powerful leaders of the globe would be there together. The notable exception was China. The Begum saw an opportunity in the event to promote a broad- based anti-China front to contain the dragon nation.

The purpose of the night culinary encounter was embedded deep down in Begum Bano was finalizing the wedding date of Adam and Parvati. She wanted it to happen sooner than later. Unknown to her, the couple had already decided. At exactly 8pm their Mercedes drove into the portico. The Begum greeted them with warm hugs. Wine session followed with Parvati relating to Mt. Kailash experiences. The tandoori chicken followed by biryani and Rogan josh was an exquisite culinary experience. A long meal but the issue of the marriage date remained unresolved. As the desserts were being served Bano had a far away look.

The Begum was at that moment thinking of the

anonymous mail from China warning her of a big Chinese conspiracy. Suddenly she got a flash of insight about the Emailer. It must be someone of noble disposition who was a high up in the Chinese Government and hence privy to the info that was being emailed to the Begum. Only one person fitted the bill. The lady minister who had met and welcomed the Begum at Beijing airport. As Adam was passing around the deserts a jingle on the Begum's mobile intimated her of another incoming mail. It was the anonymous mailer. The Begum read out the mail to an eager Adam and Parvati. It ran thus cryptically:

"Begum Bano. My greetings. China would be destroying all who attend the G8 conference of world leaders. Beware..."

13

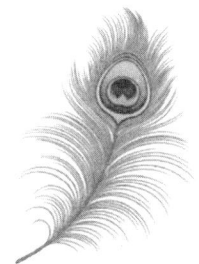

UNITY IN DIVERSITY

It was a scintillating experience that Gopal was experiencing at New York. The original plan of his flying back to India had been revised at Dr Roy's insistence and he was back in New York. The Doctor had not completed his work at the Brain Institute and wanted Gopal to be with him.

It was during his morning meditation that a trail of thought emerged from Gopal's core. Chapter 11 of the Gita deals with 'Vishwarup Darshana Yoga' or Yoga to lead an exemplary daily worldly life through be-holding the cosmic form of God. This cosmic infinite form cannot be perceived through physical eyes but only experienced by the grace of innermost divine eyes blessed to humanity by the almighty to mankind when the time came. The last revealed chapter of the Gita, namely chapter 18 ends somewhat abruptly with an assertion that wherever Krishna and Arjun will be righteousness shall prevail. The abruptness was explainable now as it was to be followed by the Secret Chapter. The secret chapter 19 enunciated the methodology of man's transcendence, Gopal knew now.

Dr. Roy had been in deep conversation with one of the monks who was narrating his deep meditative experience. He had felt a 'oneness' or a 'non-duality' with his surroundings and the electrodes attached to his skull had registered an emission of gamma rays. Dr Roy was momentarily thinking of variant gamma ray emissions from a radioactive source like the Mt Kailash phenomenon recently reported by Gopal. A gentle knock and in came Dr. Brauner the American head of the neurological institute where the experimental observations were being recorded.

Dr. Brauner was of German descent and adorned a French beard that somewhat made his sixties descend into fifties as far as age was concerned. He had a sharp intellect that analyzed and cut data inside out like a surgical knife and when coupled with his extraordinary powers of observation and deduction, he was his own solitary competitor in a strategically specialized field like the human brain's synergy with mutative meditation.

The head of the institute that Dr. Roy had selected for his research had proved worthy of the trust that had been reposed in him by the Nobel neurologist. When the American spoke, all of them including Gopal listened with rapt attention to Brauner's analysis.

He analyzed the feeling of non-duality as an expansion of pure potential awareness that was unprecedented in human brain neurology and attributed it to the synaptic brain circuits operating in powerful unison with all neurons acting as a oneness just like a laser. What had triggered this was according to Dr. Brauner was the unlocking of the Pineal gland uniting the analytical and intuitive hemispheres of the brain. Gopal was cogitating now. The monks had extraordinary inborn skills naturally developed over the years during meditation sessions dwelling on Shunyata or nothingness amidst a backdrop of compassion that had empowered them to self-unlock the gland in question to experience non duality, a primary symbol of the infinite.

It was a strange conundrum that needed an explanation.

The monks were meditating on nothingness but experiencing infinity.

Gopal was listening to Dr. Brauner intently but his mind was visualizing a scene of many millennia in the past when Krishna blessed Arjuna on the battlefield of Kurukshetra with Krishna's palm of the right hand focused towards the kneeling Arjuna's midbrain. Was Krishna activating Arjuna's pineal gland with a laser like power beam so that Arjuna's brain consciousness expands making him capable of experiencing Krishna's real infinite form.

Gopal suddenly blurted his thoughts aloud. It was Dr Roy's turn now to go into a deep meditative trance like mode. The Nobel neurologist had been struck by a thought There are rare moments when ideas come that are gateways to a revelation. This was one such query that Dr Roy could feel would be vital:

"Could the expansion of human (Arjuna's) consciousness that Krishna had brought about internally through divinity be externally induced through scientific means...?

Begum Bano who had assumed the role of de-facto UN secretary general over time, was lost in a deep thought journey sitting in her plush UN office in Downtown Dubai located in a high rise opposite to The Burj Khalifa. Adam had briefed her about the nuclear activity in Mt Kailash being clandestinely undertaken by the Chinese Government and coupled with the warning contained in the anonymous mail had triggered an alarm bell of the highest magnitude in the Bano mind. In a world full of turmoil the situation was totally unacceptable to her. People of peace were generally timid but not so The Begum. She was a determined person and was not the one to admit defeat easily. Of one thing she was sure and that was that she would never let the dragon nation succeed in its evil designs.

The anonymous mailer had given Bano a vital clue. Of course to Bano the mailer was not anonymous any longer and she was convinced that it was the Lady Minister who had welcomed her in China.

The G8 conference, since Russia's rejoining it was no longer G7, would be the location of the Chinese hideous offensive. Paris would have to be taken into confidence. What shape the holocaust would acquire was yet to be unraveled by the CIA but she would be one of the first to be briefed. Also re-assuring was a fact known only to a select few including herself. The secret American-Russian treaty uniting the two nations against The Dragon Nation duly signed by the two most popular nation's Presidents who were personally close to her and always just a Hotline away. At that instant her eyes fell on the red hotline on the left side of her desk. This is her instant link to the two most powerful people on the globe. A sudden impulse makes her press two buttons together on the Spanish red hotline appliance, something she had never done before.

A conference call with the Presidents of the two most powerful nations on the globe.

"Hello Frederick..."

"Hi Ma'am"...The American President's voice was warm and authoritative but without being offensive.

"I am trying to connect to Mikhail also..."The Begum seemed anxious.

"I am also in Madam". Interjected the Russian President suddenly.

Hearing his words the Begum continued:

"Now listen both of you, something urgent has come up that is shortly going to be an imminent threat to global peace...I have been alerted by someone senior from inside China about a possible situation.

The scenario shall unfold around the time of the G8 conclave where both of you will be present and shall be eliminated as per the Chinese sinister plan, maybe through a mega nuclear explosion. Please put both your intelligence agencies at work to decode the Chinese sinister plans. Can we all meet whenever possible since time is short so as to coordinate and finalize the preventive strategy..."

It was the American President who spoke first:

"I agree with you Madam and I am sure Prestov also"

"Yes I do Frederick

There was a consensus among all three as a sense of tense urgency gripped them.

Seeing an immediate positive response from both leaders The Begum was happy and it was decided to have a tripartite meet as suggested by the Begum exact dates to be fixed. The only thing remaining to be decided was the venue. All three uttered the venue almost simultaneously: "New Delhi. India."

14

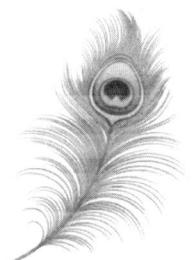

THE MENTAL MIRACLE

Adam woke up with a start.

It was 4am and the Burj was well lit up since dawn had not yet arrived. He was clutching at the remnants of the dream that he had just had and which would soon be obliterated from his memory as it usually is with dreams on waking up. Successful. He had just visioned an event emanating from his high rise office where an ultra new cell phone was being launched amidst a tumultuous sea of humanity stationed around the Burj Khalifa, the tallest man made structure on the face of the planet. It is said that dreams are made of subconscious thoughts and in the depths of his being he knew that what he had dreamt of was in fact a demanding desire that he would work to achieve shortly, he knew that. What he did not know was that the actual achievement would surpass all his expectations and would become a landmark in Human History. It is said that at times coming events reveal themselves in advance in the form of dreams and visions to empowered souls. The unfolding of subsequent facts would prove this axiom.

The same moment Adam was night dreaming Parvati was praying. She had felt a mystical ominous omen of approaching danger and she had started sobbing. A soft and gentle person, she hated violence. Her watery windows turned meditative as she kneeled to pray to ward off danger to humanity that she had intuited. Her conversation with the almighty was disrupted. A melodious caller tune. It was her loving mom Begum Bano asking her to accompany her to India after a week. The Summit between The Top leaders of Russia and America with the Begum under the auspices of the Indian President had been scheduled for New Delhi where a common strategy would be evolved to counter the Chinese silent offensive, given the latest intelligence inputs.

Parvati knew Adam would welcome her going as she could provide him vital media inputs on the summit sidelines.

Parvati was feeling thrilled to go to India once more as it would be another opportunity to meet Gopal and Dr Roy who would be at Dharamshala in the Lama's retreat to culminate their American research with the Spiritual touch. She planned to drive down for an overnight stay at Dharamshala. Gopal was in touch with her and had informed that their work in New York was coming to a close. Soon they would be at the Lama's headquarters at Dharamshala.

Strange are the ways of intertwined destinies on the vast movement of global events. Each individual was a clog in the cosmic wheel as it moved matters forward. Fate worked silently but potently in a continuous tussle with human effort.

The paths of individuals were crisis crossing on the earthly domain. Gopal knew this by now. What he had to fathom out still was the great plan behind it all since the ultimate master was nature itself.

Things were moving fast now for Parvati both professionally and personally as feelers from Adam were getting stronger for an early marriage. This was a life she looked forward to. Pleasure postponed was pleasure enhanced it was said. She suddenly felt a wave of satisfaction at the direction her life was taking with brotherly Gopal and fatherly Dr. Roy entering her life. Of course the jewel in the crown was her sweetheart Adam who had now reformed himself to become truly worthy of her.

It is bizarre that the human race is sometimes so naïve. They were the species who went beyond themselves with the evolution of countless concepts that are today fundamental to civilization and yet mankind is on the verge of self-extinction through sinister designs of evil nations who do not believe in transcending conflict but are hell bet on exhibiting their clout including nucleus to gain hegemonistic ambitions about the globe. Gopal had during rare moments of introspection realized the truth of the degrading descent of humanity during the phase of 'Kalyuga' spoken about in the ancient Hindu scriptures. The only re-assurance was that it was to be followed by a golden resurgence and transcendence of man in the 'satyuga' phase with 'Pralaya' or utter destruction structured in between. As a student of quantum physics he knew about the destruction of particles and emergence of new ones in the dance of minute constituents of matter. Einstein's space-time continuum was mystic and so was the relationship between energy and matter as in the equation $E=Mc^2$ where c was the speed of light. Gopal often grappled with such concepts where in his early dawn meditative moments science and spirituality seemed to merge and only one truth remained. It was in non-meditative moments that puzzling concepts again popped up like deadly toxins to haunt him, especially the concepts of time or 'Kaal'.

Time is supposed to be a mighty enigma. Is it moving or is it our awareness of time that moves, men have wondered. Science and scriptures have addressed these issues and the mystery apparently continues. Concepts of space, time and consciousness appear interlinked enhancing the puzzling state of affairs.

Sometimes time seems to stand still and sometimes it torrents past like a tsunami tidal wave leaving one gasping for survival. The situation was somewhat in between for Dr. Roy and Gopal with their sojourn at New York coming to a mildly satisfying conclusion. A mass of data and a number of alternative possible conclusions had emerged from their Brain Institute sojourn. The final breakthrough to activate the secret chapter however remained. Soon they would fly to the foothills of the Himalayas to be with the Lama where the spiritual dimension of their neurological quest would hopefully bring their research to the final conclusion. Gopal was looking forward to reaching Dharamshala as it would be another opportunity to meet Parvati as also His Holiness the Lama.

'Twas the night before they were to leave New York that Gopal found himself sleepless. His father had taught him the nuances of astrology and that night by a quirk of fate he found himself delving into a previously made horoscope chart of none other than Dr. Roy. His eyes suddenly expanded with amazement at the utterly bizarre combination of planets aligned in his mentor's birth date and time configuration as a momentary thought fleetingly flashed past him. He was yet to see a horoscope chart as this one despite his tinkering with thousands earlier. What Gopal was gazing at right in front of him was a unique configuration of planets in the astrological chart spread out on his bed.

Astrology was a science in itself as Gopal had slowly but surely realized. What was missing were accurate experts who could delve into the charts of individuals to extract meaning from them.

Although he was very young when he had interacted with his grandfather on a couple of occasions discussing matters beyond horoscopes, he still vividly recalled that wintry night when Dadu, as he affectionately addressed his Grandpa, opening up a stranger's horoscope and guided him to look for the position of Uranus in the chart. This would uplift the horoscope chart value beyond a single lifetime to the travel of a soul across several lifetimes. Gopal came out of his memory trance with his Dadu and as his eyes focused on hunting the Uranus position in Dr. Roy's chart, understanding dawned.

Uranus was bang in the Centre of the chart spread out before him with nine planets in concentric circles around it, making a total of ten including the contemporary Planet X that astronomy had unearthed. Time and again Gopal had experienced this strange partnership between Science and Scriptures that seemed to be utterly in union to empower humanity. Once again right before his eyes the dance of the 10 planets seemed to shriek out a vital message to the horoscope reader. "Dadu, bless me!" Gopal seemed to be now talking to his Grandpa. Lo and behold, a mental miracle surpassing deductive thought occurred. He had to his own utter astonishment decoded the vital message from the planetary testament and that too in a flash.

Dr. Roy's soul travels would engulf ten lifetimes, each more vital than the previous one.

15

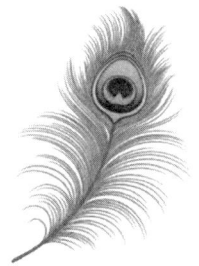

Tying Loose Ends

Depression it is said is the inability to create a future—a kind of visible darkness in the state of mind that comes like an uninvited guest of sorts. It was in the recent couple of years that a feeling of temporary lows had started creeping into her psyche whenever the outside world intruded into her inner peace. Of course Noor was well aware of this and now knew how to deal with it. Ever since the death of her life mate living behind his love symbol, the sweet girl child Parvati, Bano had been often battered by such obnoxious bouts of fear and uncertainty resulting in a sour sorrow surreptitiously surrounding her entire being. Yoga had been her savior. Many times she had felt the need for a companion more for the sake of a secure complete world for her daughter. However, as she delivered into the world of diplomacy the void was filled slowly but surely ably empowered by the grit and gut of a beautiful but strong offspring. The entry of Adam had put all her fears at rest and today she could wholeheartedly dedicate her endeavors to world peace and development.

Madame Lee, China's culture minister, woke up early that cloudy morning in Beijing. The clouds were dark and low and rain was expected any moment. The politburo meeting with Chairman Zing himself presiding would begin in 2 hours at the party headquarters and so Lee had to hurry. No agenda for the meet had been specified but the minister had a strong inkling that something very significant was in the offing. She would be proved right soon.

It was at sharp 9 A.M. that Chairman Zing, dressed in his customary deep blue with red Chinese collar suit, called the meeting to order. It had started raining outside and the sound of thunder seemed to match the Chairman's vociferous monologue. One look around and Lady Lee could see that the entire cabinet was there and soon the agenda became clear.

The Chairman was speaking in a somewhat egoistic tone of the superiority of the Great People's Republic of China. Madame Ching Lee could feel a wave of haughtiness rising in the Supremo. The others listened with rapt attention. The time had come for the globe to acknowledge that Beijing would rule the world. The purpose of the meet was to prepare the top leadership to carry out a public relations exercise and each cabinet member would be allotted a specific world region to visit and spread the message of friendship. At this juncture The Chairman burst out in a short grunt of cunning satisfaction. He was on an auto-thinking spree as he was used to when in a megalomaniac mood. The message of friendship would be an effective camouflage for the real attack on the psychology of other nations that they were weak. The monstrosity that would be unleashed on the vital place at the vital time would bring the world on its knees.

The Dragon would rule the globe.

Lady Lee was at that same moment thinking about the e-mail she had sent to Begum Bano, albeit anonymously. She knew the mail had been delivered and also realized that Bano had no means to contact her. The ministers assembled were listening to their Chairman with rapt attention as he spoke on his vision for the People's Republic. The Chinese cabinet was now aware that an offensive was in the offing and looked forward to further details.

No luck. The Chairman would not share any details further to ensure secrecy and the meeting concluded curtly. When all had gone and Lady Lee was about to exit she heard the Chairman's harsh tone:

"Lady Minister, please step inside for a moment. I have some urgent instructions for you…"

He wanted her to go to a country (within the coming week) and her visit would play a vital role. The need of the hour was to extend the hand of friendship with this country and Lady Lee would be able to do it as always, expediency was the ultimate guide and selfishness the best pathway to attain China's ambitions or so believed the leader of this near-rogue nation. The Chairman emphasized the significance of Lady's mission. It was an important nation she was being asked to visit and build solid bridges of friendship, he remarked emphatically.

The nation was none other than India.

It is said that sometimes life can be a pleasure and at others an ordeal. Getting up early in the morning was an ordeal for Dr. Roy since the flight was at 5 A.M. but the prospect of meeting The Lama was definitely a pleasure more so with Gopal by his side. Somehow he had developed a fondness for the young boy bordering on a fatherly aura. They had been together for time enough to understand their nuanced relationship. Gopal from his side looked upon Dr. Roy as a mentor.

Dr. Roy had completed his work at the Brain Institute and he knew the final conclusion would be achieved at Dharamshala and then Dubai. It would be at Dubai that the loose ends would be tied securely, Gopal had predicted. His mentor had started believing in matters beyond the scope of science.

Many things Gopal had told about the neurologist's past were true and hence the belief that what he would tell for the future would also be correct. They both looked forward to the re-Union with the Lama as they boarded from New York.

The flight landed at Delhi Airport on time and they proceeded towards the helipad to take a chartered chopper to Dharamshala courtesy Adam. Soon they would be in the foothills of the Himalayas and Gopal looked forward to the experience of the fresh breeze of the mountains. Somehow the heights made Gopal's neurons run faster leading to a heightened streamlined functioning. It was a quirk of fate

TYING LOOSE ENDS

that Parvati would be landing in Delhi and would be visiting them for a short while in Dharamshala while her mom, Begum Bano, would be busy with the summit between the two top leaders.

Their chopper landed at Dharamshala and the representative of His Holiness was there to receive them. Soon they landed on the helipad adjacent to the residence of The Lama and as they were being ushered in Gopal saw a group of about 20 monks meditating in a hall which they bypassed as they were directed to an inner chamber.

The massive teak door opened and there they were in the divine presence of a sweet soul. He welcomed Dr. Roy with a warm embrace as Gopal touched his feet. The visitors could feel his aura as they squatted to face him while he was reading a short prayer with folded hands.

The Lama was the one who started speaking as he looked towards The neurologist:

"So how was your trip to The United States, Doctor."

"Your Holiness thanks to you we had the opportunity to work with our American counterparts and empower ourselves with the latest knowledge and research on the working of the human brain. The next aspiration is to get that crucial breakthrough maybe from the spiritual angle as Gopal says and hence this visit to see the lamas meditate."

Dr Roy's voice trailed as he looked at Gopal. The Lama put in the final word:

"You are most welcome to be here and please feel free to ask for anything. Whenever you want to meet me you can walk in any time. I wish both of you the very best of luck in your endeavors. A very good night to you..."

16

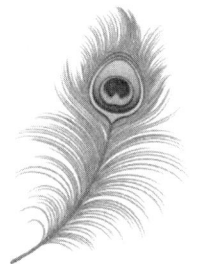

The Cryptic Contact

Begum Noor Bano had many things on her mind as the Air Bus had a soft landing at Indira Gandhi International Airport of New Delhi. It was a clear sunny sky as clear as the Begum's resolve to solve the urgent issue at hand. Bano was a lady of peace but had resolved to adopt all means to contain the Dragon. Soon President Taylor and President Prestov would be landing for the summit to be held in her presence under the auspices of the Indian Prime Minister Dr. Lakshmi Pandit. The venue was the Presidential Residence designed by the famous British architect Lutyens.

As the Begum entered the VIP lounge on landing, her heart missed a beat. There in front of her was Madame Lee who was visiting Delhi at her Chairman's request. The two ladies rushed towards each other and during the embrace the Chinese lady just had time enough to whisper something in the Begum's ear before she was whisked away by her Chinese security men. Bano managed to keep a calm face but her mind was in turmoil at The Chinese minister of culture's whispered words:

"Contact me today...Please..."

All leaders including Taylor, Petrov, The Begum as well as Madame Lee were staying at The Sheraton, Delhi amidst tight security as the Summit was slated to begin in 2 hours time. The Director CIA would also be in the American delegation. Bano was all formally dressed up soon and while in the washroom had devised a way to contact Madame Lee. She picked up the hotel hotline and straightaway called the reception to enquire about the Chinese minister's room number after introducing herself curtly.

It was 212 a floor below hers. She then rang for room service and instructed the girl to deliver a short sealed written note to room 212 discreetly and bring back an answer.

The note was concealed in a bouquet of flowers. The directness of the method worked and soon Begum had in front of her Lee's delicately hand-written note which read as follows:

"Respected Begum Bano,

Destiny has given me the final chance to warn humanity of the evil designs of our top Chinese leadership through you. What was a suspicion in my mind has now been confirmed. The venue and time of the carnage to be unleashed by our rogue nation has been confirmed by my reliable sources. It will be at the inauguration of the G8 in Paris, which has only a few months to go. An explosion, a hundred times more powerful than the first atomic bomb, would rock the entire city and kill all the world leaders immediately assembled for the event including the American and Russian Presidents. Please Begum...Do Something."

THE CRYPTIC CONTACT

The earnest appeal at the end of the note was disturbing as Bano weighed her options. At this moment the Hotline came alive that she had to now walk towards the summit hall. The Begum approached the decorated door and entered the inner lobby teething with security. Two Indian army men decorated with gala try medals opened the doorway to the chamber of the summit. Three people rose to greet her. They were the Indian, the Russian and the American Leaders who would now huddle together to face the gravest man-made disaster the globe had to face."

Adam hated being alone but whenever loneliness was thrust upon him his mind somehow ultimately got activated and the bizarre consequence was 'out of box 'thinking. A sense of satisfaction had enveloped him ever since he had sponsored the research project led by Dr. Roy. He knew that it would have far reaching consequences. What he could never have imagined was that one day he would become a vital catalyst in bringing an awesome transcendent era to humanity.

Global Media Inc. had recently added a mobile telephony division with in-house staff researching various apps. The decision was commercial but an elevated thought was arising in him. An inner feeling told him that perhaps one day this division would conjoin with Dr. Roy's research to unfold and activate the secret chapter of the Gita to mankind. Mobile telephony had reached new business heights in recent years and besides the function of communication new dimensions and innovations had sprung up utilizing the basic mobile technology. This involved the development of various apps which could be put to a variety of usages for contemporary humans.

Adam's dawn thoughts were interrupted by a shrill ring on his private hotline. Only a select few had this number including Parvati. He knew it had to be her at this hour and promptly picked it up. A sweet voice spoke up:

"Hi Babe, I am driving down to Dharamshala to meet His Holiness and catch up with Dr. Roy and Gopal...Mom is busy at the summit...What news at your end..."

There was a brief gap before Adam replied:

"Remembering you Darling...it's good you are going...I was thinking why don't you take an interview with The Lama for our global magazine...you know His Holiness has become a most popular personality for media houses around the globe..."

"Excellent idea..."

"And one more thing...this time when you are back our holiday is overdue..."

A girlish giggle and she signed off with the customary words:

"Bye for now...luv u..."

"Luv u too"

Adam's reply was short and sweet and ended abruptly as his chief advisor on mobiles entered and both were lost in a long technical inter action.

The hills appeared majestic to Parvati as she closed the mobile. The Private Uber cab was proceeding on the undulating road among the lush greenery. She was getting a subconscious intuition of being a part of a human network that would lead to something vital. Her mind at that juncture was at two places with Adam and with her mom. Adam she had just talked to and her concern was the summit at Delhi going on at this very hour. She wished her mom success for the summit and sincerely hoped that the Chinese menace would be contained and peace would prevail on their precious planet. Coupled with this desire was a tingling expectancy of a pleasure fast approaching. The joy of meeting Gopal and Dr. Roy along with the Lama was overwhelming.

The fast moving landscape in the hills as visible from the cab window made a subconscious trail of thought emerge in Parvati's mind. Life was moving at a steady pace now with Adam in her life. The tingling sensation of a young girl about to be a bride was not imaginary. A true-life mate would surely be hers now. She felt she deserved this. Her emotive thoughts were galloping ahead now. A bonny boy and then a giggling girl slowly emerged on her mental landscape. The cab gathered speed and she back into the present with bang, holding on to her tan knap sack securely. Fantasies she knew turned into facts sometimes. As the crisp mountain air infiltrated her, she suddenly felt a new surge of energy and excitement of what lay ahead in her life. It made her sink back in her rear seat to plunge her into a short and sweet slumber.

17

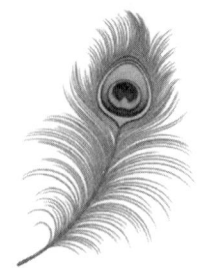

GATEWAY TO INFINITY

As the three leaders rose to greet Begum Bano she enthusiastically responded as they settled down along the round table. It was the Indian Prime Minister who spoke first and welcomed all of them stating that it was her nation's rare privilege to play host to the summit. She invited Begum to conduct the proceedings then onwards. Bano got up instantly and spoke gently but firmly:

"Friends, we are gathered here for a specific purpose and at the outset let me share vital information."

The Begum then revealed the entire episode of Madame Lee. President Taylor at once confirmed that The Director CIA had put up a secret report also to this effect. Prestov looked concerned and urged all to take coordinated action to prevent this mishap. The detailed deliberations lasted a full 4 hours with key aides joining. The Director of the CIA was asked by Frederick to brief about Mt. Kailash episode. At the end of it all a comprehensive plan to execute a coordinated Intel based action was agreed upon. A multinational Para military task force would be constituted ASAP with the aim of gathering intelligence and nullifying the Chinese plan and defusing the nuclear offensive to be launched at the G8 summit. It was during the one day deliberations that The anti-China pact was revealed to her officially by the American and Russian leaders. The Begum through her personal diplomacy had ensured a united front of nations to counter the Chinese threat. The combined power of the two superpowers would go a long way to ensure global peace and development.

Of course the dragon nation was a force to reckon with on its own but the united front had many advantage points in its favour.

As she looked around the hall with satisfaction Bano's thought was to Lady Lee who too was in Delhi. The lady at that time was interacting with her counterpart at the Indian Ministry of Culture. The Begum was wondering as to why the Chairman of the People's Republic had deputed Lee to Delhi to coincide with the Summit. The timing troubled and intrigued her. One fact was clear to her that The Chinese leader was the most cunning of all global leaders and all his moves had a sinister deadly design behind it.

At the formal luncheon at the end of the summit all the leaders appeared satisfied and a bit relieved at their timely action plan. The American President appeared relaxed as he sought the Russian counterpart's advice on how to lose weight and appear sexy. The relaxed joking over Vodka was nice. Of course the most satisfied was Begum who had finally succeeded in bringing together the top global leadership now committed to peace. The Begum shook hands with the two Presidents and turned to the Charismatic Indian Prime Minister looking resplendent in her sober lavender coloured silk saree.

As the leaders were leaving the summit venue The Begum got a call from an unlisted number. It was Madame Lee anxious to know the summit outcome. The Begum just replied in two words before closing the mobile:

"All Well..."

Parvati felt enthralled in the pine hills of Dharamshala. The morning air had a vitality due to the freshness and as she walked towards the living quarters of Dr. Roy and Gopal, she could hear the early morning chanting by a hundred monks and their resounding deep bass seemed to penetrate inside her. It had a catalytic effect on her whole being as she rang the gong to the residential quarters. A junior monk opened the door and ushered her in pointing to a multi coloured teak door presumably the entry to Dr. Roy's room. She knew he would be expecting her. The monk knocked twice on the door and it was opened from the inside by none other than Gopal.

Parvati rushed to greet him and they hugged warmly as she commented that he had put on since the last time they had met. He merely grinned. Dr Roy beckoned them to enter and she gave him a tight embrace. The neurologist enquired about the interview with The Lama and she affirmed that she would be completing it during the afternoon when she would be meeting His Holiness and was sure it was going to be fantastic. The chanting by the Lamas in the adjoining hall continued. It was a part of further research that the Nobel neurologist was conducting, Gopal explained. Once a start has been made, the rest tends to follow. Events moved by destiny since the day of the Nobel presentation were reaching a conclusion it seemed to Gopal and he shared this with Parvati. The green tea gave instant energy to all of them it seemed and just as they were about to wind up the session, a Lama of tender age came to inform them that the meditation of the monks was about to end and Dr. Roy was required urgently. Gopal and Dr. Roy got up to leave as Parvati asked if she could join. They welcomed her. All got up together and entered the adjoining room where the chanting was receding to a peaceful echo of its original crescendo. The electrodes connecting the brain implants and the measuring instruments were in place and Dr. Roy would now analyze them.

It was a largish hall where the monks were assembled and their brain activity was being monitored. The moment Dr. Roy entered the hall coincided with the conclusion of the chanting. The technician took the readings of the brain activity to the neurologist as the monks filed out. Amazing was the feeling that enraptured Dr. Roy.

The observations at the New York brain institute stood doubly confirmed now.

As the learned neurologist's gaze fell on the graphs that showed the very high oscillation rates of the vibrations of the monks' brains he let out a grunt of surprise. The monks in a brain state of wholeness were emitting Gamma waves. Apparently as per Dr. Roy's observations Gamma Rays had the ability to unify the entire cortex...the whole brain became one unified singularity devoid of all divisions. Such conditions gave a sense of infinite wholeness to the experience of the brain and had resulted from the monks indulging in a meditation with compassion. The resultant expansion of consciousness towards a whole infinite entity was exactly the state of being indicated in the secret chapter of the Gita. Alas this kind of brain state was apparently available to Tibetan monks. The challenge before the learned neurologist was how to make this state available to normal humans.

A strange thought took Dr. Roy captive. If a singularity brain state led to gamma rays emission could it be possible that an intake of gamma rays by the brain induce such an infinite feeling of wholeness in the human brain and expand and empower its experience. Normally converse conditions are held. Could it just be possible in this situation...

The Lama beamed as Parvati entered his sanctum sanctorum for a video interview. The initial formalities over she fired her first Salvo:

"Holiness, what are your thoughts on the human mind?" He cleared his throat, smiled and with childlike expressions answered spoke up benevolently. "The human mind is the most awesome gift given to mankind with its billions of neurons working in unison to solve the toughest of dilemmas in its subtle role of a life coach. The skill of using one's mind to gain a clear overview of complex situations to solve human problems is awesome, Parvati. Mind is the ultimate weapon that triggers and helps unleash the limitless potential in any individual bringing enrichment, success and satisfaction. Success is the light at the end of a tunnel and this thought motivates".

Parvati's interjection at this stage is sudden.

"What other role besides the above do you visualize for the human brain, your Holiness".

The Lama closed his eyes momentarily and proceeded:

"Parvati, the human mind, remember always, is the ultimate gateway to the infinite or as some would say God. The harmony and the compassion with exclusion of brain thoughts slowly and steadily helps man experience nothingness or 'shunyata' where man is one within so practice it and see for yourself my young crusader"

A few more questions and the interview were over but Parvati knew that the gems of thought from Lama were priceless.

Destiny was vigorously at work now involving her in a mega way in global affairs ever since Adam had entered in her life.

At that very moment she could feel herself as a very small spec but a very dynamic one in the infinite scheme of things called cosmos.

18

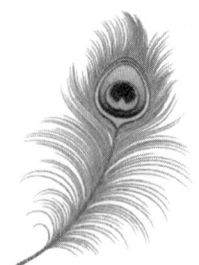

THE DOUBLE AGENT

As Parvati was experiencing herself as a dynamic spec in Dharamshala, an interesting interlude was unfolding itself in Dubai. Adam was at an overnight stay for a Global Media CEO's conference from ten nations to deliberate on the role of media in the contemporary world scenario. The 'Global Media Person' award for the year was also to be announced. It was Adam's futuristic address that won the day climaxing in his winning the coveted award of 'Global Media Person' of that year. The world had once again acknowledged him as The King in the Media Arena.

It was at the glittering cocktails at the 7 star ship shaped hotel, that he met her in her official capacity of CEO American Media Conglomerate that full moon night. With Parvati away, Adam was somewhat a lonely man personally that night despite the public adulation. She approached him first.

"Hi Adam, I'm Sherry Donovan...Congratulations for your award."

He turned to see a ravishing beauty in a glittering see-through black gown with Spanish red accessories matched down to the high stilettos, the designer Vuitton bag and the gorgeous lipstick. He too was human and she was game. The sweet resultant shift from the party venue to his deluxe apartment was swift and thoughtless. Physical attraction often shuts the mental valves of the human mind momentarily but the regret is prolonged. The abrupt mutual undressing process was suddenly frozen as Adam's eyes fell on the sparkling diamond ring on his Venus finger of the left hand engagement gift from Parvati. It had sheer power of commitment radiating from the sparks acting as an awesomely powerful pulsar message of loyalty. Providence was with Parvati that night.

Adam had put on back his clothes and suddenly walked out leaving a totally nonplussed sherry back in the room all alone.

Moments make up a lifetime and some moments come surreptitiously and in some cases repetitively seemingly conveying a message from the core of one's being. It was one such moment that Roy experienced during his siesta that afternoon. Suddenly he had been transported onto a battlefield in which two armies faced each other and the bugle for battle was being sounded. He saw the blood, he heard the painful cry of the wounded and he could smell the rotten stench of dead human bodies all littered around. Then in a flash it was over and he woke up thrilled about his present experimentation on the human brain.

When Dr. Roy was excited about the gamma rays in Dharamshala and the experiments in America that had revealed that the pineal gland deactivation was part of a wholesome brain experience, at that self-same moment The Begum was catching an Emirates flight back to Dubai from New Delhi. Events were moving fast but she was glad that contact had been established with Madame Lee. The Russian American pact had been activated and their joint Intel and action would help contain the dragon now.

The Begum had the unlisted number of Madame Lee and they had promised to maintain contact. As she remembered the Chinese lady culture minister, so too Lady Lee was remembering The Begum as she was being driven straight to the Chairman's residence from the airport in Beijing for reporting on her India visit. The security was tight around the Chairman's office as usual she observed as she was led into the Chairman's personal office and asked to wait. Hardly a minute had elapsed that The Chairman of the People's Republic entered in his customary semi-military uniform, looking as pompous as ever.

The meeting with The Chairman was short and crisp.

After hearing Madame Lee briefly he did most of the talking:

"Good work Lee...You have done an excellent job...You have now gained the confidence of The Begum and through her the leaders of Russia and America. What you feed them with will be easily digested by them now."

Lady Lee looked happy and was feeling tense in the solitary company of her esteemed Chairman as he patted her on the back and continued addressing her:

"The Republic is proud of you, Lee."

Lee was thrilled beyond words as she added:

"Yes Hon Chairman, now they truly believe that the holocaust will come from a nuclear explosion at the G8. Little do they know about our secret plan that will make all vital world leaders literally become dust much earlier at the Dubai expo in a manner so different from the nuclear blast technique."

The Chairman stepped forward and clasped her hand tightly indicating that the meeting had ended. Madame Lee walked out with her head held high. That day being appreciated as a most patriotic lady by the Chairman himself was the happiest moment of her life.

Begum Noor Banu could never in her wildest dreams have imagined that Lady Lee was a double agent and a spy.

The headquarters of the CIA is the George Bush Centre for Intelligence situated at Langley, Virginia. A high level event was in progress that sunny day attended by a select few people urgently summoned. These were the agents looking after the Special Division or covert operations of the most efficient Intelligence agency in the world.

The atmosphere in the situation room at the CIA headquarters was tense as the Director along with his senior agents listened with rapt attention to their special agent from

Beijing. The term 'special agent' was a contemporary adaptation of the term 'spy' in vogue around the Second World War.

The Covert undisclosed agent was playing a secret video recording of a clandestine Air Force facility somewhere on the border between China and Russia. The clip had been made by a mole of the CIA and was of Chinese origin. In the clip, an instructor was lecturing a group of senior level pilots judging from their uniforms simultaneously pointing to some prototypes of some hazy mini planes. The instructor's voice could be heard clearly in Chinese, which the CIA agent was translating into English simultaneously for the Director. The Chinese instructor's words ran something like this:

"Comrades, please listen carefully. Our intelligence agent who is part of the cabinet has successfully misled the enemy leaders of America and Russia about an attack that would occur from our side on the occasion of the G 8 conference of world leaders. However the real date and venue are in fact different. The place is Dubai and the time is much earlier than the G8 conference, comrades. At the appointed moment we will start our Operation Victory as the World Expo 2025 is being jointly inaugurated at Dubai by the top leaders of the so called top 5 nations namely America, Russia, Britain, France and India. Comrades, they will pay heavily for omitting China. The moment the flags of the 5 nations are unfurled, our drones will hit their targets. The genetic profiles of the 5 leaders have already been factored into the drone's target simulation.

There will be no way that the 5 drones will not destroy and bring about the total annihilation of the 5 leaders since the drones have been irrevocably programmed to do so. There will be no collateral damage. As the leaders are eliminated the resultant global chaos will make our stable nation the undisputed Emperor of the Globe."

The video continued to dole out specific instructions about the operation based upon artificial intelligence technology developed by China in the field of sophisticated drones. Instantly 'Tiger' deputed the Assistant Director of the CIA to analyze and submit an immediate strategy to counter and nullify the Dragon drone horror. One thing remained. The President had to be informed immediately. The Director entered his private office and picking up the red hotline literally spit out the words:

"Mr. President, there is an emergency..."

19

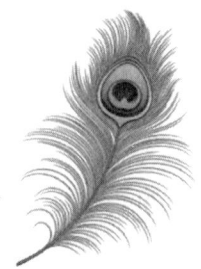

TECHNO-SPIRITUALITY

It is said that if man takes one step towards nature then Nature takes ten steps towards humanity. Adam was the fulcrum unknown to him that would activate man's single step towards the upliftment of humanity and be reciprocated ten-fold through the blooming of his research vision through the new mobile initiative his mega global corporation was presently engaged in.

Adam had rather nonchalantly been grossed in his thoughts the major part of the day and had just asked his team for a meeting at noon that very day regarding the apps which would form part of the new brand of mobiles his corporation was to launch at the inauguration of the Expo. It was at that moment that Dr. Roy called him up and shared the info regarding the gamma rays phenomena. They were acting in complete unison as a dynamic team now. Speaking in a rather urgent tone the neurologist added:

"Adam, I was just thinking of the possibility of the converse hypothesis whereby we can induce gamma rays into the human brain to make it experience wholeness. Can this be done maybe through some technology connected with mobiles? A technology or maybe an app based on meditation techniques of Buddhist monks that can provide inputs to the open ended dendrites of the brain after deactivating the pineal gland to achieve our goal?"

"Dr. Roy I have called a meeting of my entire mobile team and shall put them on the job in this direction. Shall revert."

A moment pause and then Adam's persuasive voice added:

"Dr. I have a request to make. Would it be possible for you to brief my technical team about what you shared with me just now.

I have instructed my team to assemble at noon today to discuss the App research progress. Do join us please..."

The neurologist looked at his watch as he answered:

"Adam, my pleasure and privilege, I shall be there."

"Thanks and bye for now".

At sharp noon 13 suit clad men entered the conference room adjacent to Adam's office. Adam was already there and began the proceedings with a short introduction about Dr. Roy who entered at that moment. Adam straightaway asked the Nobel neurologist to take over the mic. Dr. Roy looked around at the assembled men before proceeding. His voice tone was matter of fact:

"Gentlemen,

Adam has already introduced me and I thank him for his kind words. Today, I bring a challenge for you, a vital task that seeks to uplift our very existence on the globe as a human race."

Dr. Roy then proceeded to narrate the whole story of their exploration till date. He had spoken at length and was a little out of breath at the end but looking at the enthralled faces of his audience he felt he had conveyed the essence of his quest and was hence experiencing contentment.

The chief of Apps division spoke up almost immediately as Dr. Roy concluded:

"Sir, there are basically two input senses available to have a penetrative influence within the brain namely audio and visual technology...Gamma rays can be induced in the brain cortex by a suitable catalytic prompter activated through a super-sensitive App. utilizing the brain entry pathways at the precise frequencies through the ears or eyes depending on which methodology we choose to reach out to the micro-neurons of the human brain. Also we could research on a combination of audio-visual inputs to have the desired results."

Adam had been listening with rapt attention now responded enthusiastically:

"Excellent analysis Charles...go for it...but time is short...give me deadlines."

"40 days sir starting today...we will meet on the 41st day and I am dead sure our team will come up with something..."

TECHNO-SPIRITUALITY

"Ok...thanks all. The meeting is closed..."

Adam spoke in a matter of fact tone.

Later that evening three men met at Adam's office. Dr Roy was speaking and Adam and Gopal were listening:

"Gentlemen, it is good we are meeting for we are short of time. Gamma waves are the fastest documented brainwave range that oscillates between 30 to 100 Hertz. In New York we observed a relationship between such waves and a unity of consciousness, which is a stepping stone to an awareness of infinity. Adam, your Apps team has to induce such gamma waves into the brain core to empower it for the above experience just as Krishna did for Arjun on the battlefield of Kurukshetra."

Adam responded almost instantly:

"Dr Roy, my initial brainstorming with my apps team earlier today is rather encouraging. I have given them your research note on the subject and they propose to experiment on the induction of such waves into the brain through the audio-visual pathway. This would deactivate the divisive pineal gland and the brain would be ready to experience an infinite like experience through the open ended dendrites acting as inlets from the vast unlimited consciousness that holds the entire creation as revealed by contemporary cosmologists now."

Gopal could see the high level of dedication of the two men. His astrological intuition had already given him a positive indication on the matter. Soon the time will be at hand.

Adam remained back alone in the plush conference room overlooking the Burj Khalifa.

He had a puzzled expression on his handsome face as he cogitated on the enormity of the task at hand. He could see that he was a spec in a vast infinite conundrum but each spec mattered just as each wave combined together became the Ocean. The ecstasy of impending success overtook him as it does most dreamers as a crazy thought wave engulfed him: 'What if we succeed?"

Begum Noor had just retired for the night when she woke up with a start. The Director of the CIA was on the line. He wished her a very good morning and then proceeded to brief her about the Chinese camouflage and the secret drones plan. Begum was shattered when he said that Madame Lee was a mole placed in their camp to mislead them. The Director assured her that the counter offensive was being launched and he would be briefing her continuously. He concluded by conveying good wishes from the President of the United States of America and from his own side for the Begum and of course Parvati.

Time is the biggest shock absorber and a few hours later Begum Bano was up and about in her UN office getting in touch with all the top leaders and updating them as per the Director's request. Events had temporarily shaken up the non-Chinese camp no doubt but they were all thanking their stars that Madame Lee's subterfuge had been unmasked in time. The Begum, on a sudden impulse, rang up her daughter and shared the update. Parvati was shaken momentarily but regained her posture almost immediately. The thought of the dinner get-together was comforting where Dr. Roy and her mom would be meeting for the first time along with Adam and Parvati. She knew that Dr. Roy and Adam were having a vital meeting that very minute with the mobile staff at Adam's office. It was satisfying that Dr. Roy had completed his work at Dharamshala and with the blessings of The Lama had returned to Dubai.

It was at 9 P.M. that the four of them assembled at the exclusive Armani Hotel in downtown Dubai. As Parvati introduced Dr. Roy to her mom she could feel the warmth of the hug that the neurologist gave to The Begum dressed in her customary flowing robe of a light lilac hue. Dr. Roy was praising Parvati to her mom as Adam nodded profusely. The evening was refreshing for all but one was missing. Parvati picked up her mobile and invited the missing person and there he was almost in no time. Gopal was welcomed warmly by all and then the party began and lasted till the wee hours of the morning. The climax came when Dr. Roy asked for a dance with the Begum and she agreed much to the surprise of her daughter.

The waltz was soft and it was Noor and Laik who became rather oblivious to everything and enjoyed it. Gopal was busy explaining astrology to Adam who seemed impressed and Parvati was engrossed in all of them. What an evening she was thinking. They were like a family now...all of them and the feeling gave her a sense of security that had crept in ever since her Dad's demise when she was hardly ten.

Today she had a father figure and a brother and of course her mom too.

It was only the sudden culmination to the music that made the party come to an end.

As they took leave of each other the thought in Dr. Roy's mind was:

"Why did I not meet Begum Bano earlier?"

20

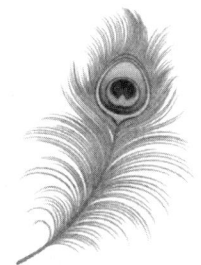

Eureka

It was a few weeks before Dr. Roy came in touch with Charles that the following sequence of events had occurred.

The Sahara mall is a shopping cum eating hub sandwiched between the emirates of Dubai and Sharjah. It was on the dot at 6pm that Parvati spotted her love sitting alone on a corner table wearing tinted shades and a golfer's cap. A crude attempt to be incognito. Parvati took a chair bang opposite and ordered a vanilla frappe. Then she waited. Adam was looking at his Rolex when a discreet cough alerted him. A man in his mid-thirties was extended his hand

"I'm Charles...pleased to meet you Mr Gore..."

He pulled up a chair uninvited as Adam obliged with a brief handshake. Parvati had already started her assigned discreet filming activity. She could see that the visitor had Charles' complete attention. She was right. Charles was revealed as the head of cellular technology of Aerotel Inc. a leading multinational next only to Adam's conglomerate and was offered the post after Francis the incumbent had joined Adam's Global Media Inc. He had a strange tale to tell.

"Mr. Gore it was at 7 P.M. just the day before Francis died that I got a call from him to meet him at the viewing tower at the Burj Khalifa. I arrived in time to witness a nervous Francis gasping for breath and furtively looking around. We could see the city's landscape with all the splendour of lights from the 'Top' as the place was called. Francis told me flatly that his life was in danger.as a rogue faction from his former employees wanted him to hand over his recent research on a special App he was on the verge of cracking on the design board for Global Media Inc. It was going to be a groundbreaking invention with global ramifications. Then without a word Francis thrust a USB in my hands and literally vanished saying that it was all there...the next morning came the news of his suicide but I knew it was murder but for obvious reasons I did not go to the police...'

Adam had been listening intently and now interjected :

"What did you find in the USB, Charles ?..."

Charles glanced around and continued:

"The data was humongous...It was a marvel of a 7 pronged App. The first 6 levels were fully documented and functional theoretically. Only the crucial final 7th phase remained that would lead to the stunning climax for the user.

On seeing Adam's impatient face Charles continued:

"Sir, the app was based on the opening up of the so called 7 Chakras of the human body that find mention in ancient Yoga. Each phase of the App represents a particular Chakra

EUREKA

and here I must explain what the Chakra word means.

Chakras are the circular vortexes of energy that are placed on different parts of the human spinal cord conveying life energy or 'Prana' and are linked to various organs and glands. They have to be awakened one by one in a particular order from the base of the solar plexus to the crown in the brain.

Francis had synchronised the first six in cellular terms and was on the edge of the final."

Adam interrupted him abruptly :

"What is the final take, Charles ?..."

"Yes sir, I was coming to that...Francis was positive that once the final Chakra was decoded in cellular terms it would have stupendous implications. Let me conclude by repeating Francis' last sentence where he states that we are knocking on the final 7th doorway to empower humanity to experience the taste of infinity..."

Saying this Charles got up to leave and suddenly handed him a USP saying it is all there. Adam's parting words amazed Charles.

"Charles, you are hereby appointed as head of the Cellular division of my corporation to finish what Francis had begun...welcome on board..."

There were three pairs of moist eyes in the Sahara Food Court at that moment including those of Parvati who had filmed the entire meeting between the two men.

Ever since Charles had taken over as head of Cellular

Division of Global Media Inc a fresh wave of inspiring dedication had gripped him together with a steadfast

Determination to complete what Francis had begun. To begin with he analyzed that the chronological unfolding of the 7 chakras in cellular terms involved the linkage at each level one by one in order like climbing a ladder rung by rung till you reach the last step, the pinnacle. Francis had synchronised the first 6 steps but before he could unravel the last one he was eliminated. A sense of outrage acted as a catalyst and Charles was determined to complete it and had Adam's full support although he was unaware of the details.

Mobile technology had been basically used for cellular communication and with the coming of the new millennium a standard mobile device took shape as a mobile phone, Gps navigator, web browser, instant messenger and a gaming console. Soon came the Apps and the tools for mobile App development like Appcelerator based on various web technologies and a music visualiser based on extracting waveform and frequency info and interpolating it with visual data. Charles was constantly on his work station in the pursuit of finalising what had begun. It was at this stage that Adam introduced him to Dr. Roy who provided him the vision of his own endeavours. The Nobel neurologist acted as a wild energiser for Charles to add human neurone experience to cellular app refinement to seek the purest form of techno-human experience merger of the highest order.

Francis had already synchronised each of the six chakras in his multi app. on the basis of inputting optimum frequencies for each particular chakra controlling various human organs. It was just like 6 flowers blooming one by one ready to welcome the final climaxing seventh namely the Sahasrara or crown chakra in the brain. Once the tip off threshold was reached, the mystical human brain would be empowered to the highest infinite experience. The crown chakra was often referred to as a thousand petalled Lotus and was related to the human Kundalini, the energy of consciousness imploding to enable the 'samadhi' experience in the human brain. This was identical to what Dr. Roy had expounded in neurological terms in his presentation and Charles now knew the pathway to success. Dr Roy had also referred to R. Davidson's experiment at the University of Wisconsin where EEG electrodes had been attached to Buddhist monks meditating on 'compassion and unconditional love' and recorded their non-finite experience accompanied by emission of 40 cycles per second frequency Gamma Rays with oscillation of 40 cycles per second. The Nobel neurologist had pointed out an interesting challenge to Charles when he propounded a startling proposition. If a non-finite human brain experience could emit Gamma Rays would the converse hold true namely if Gamma Rays of the desired frequency were somehow fed into the brain maybe through the open ended dendrites through an app based cellular technology, what would be the result. Charles had accepted Dr Roy's challenge silently.

It was a full moon night and Charles was hooked up to an audio visualizer from the mobile prototype soon to be launched by Global Inc. He was today venturing for the first time into the 7th stage after completely accomplishing the first six chakra-cellular sync. The vital input in the 7th stage was the feeding of the Gamma oscillations at 40 cycles per second into the human neurological sensation. Hardly the 7th part of the App was run for 30 seconds Charles could feel an exotic experience of endless joy and unity with the infinite universe. Unknown to him his open ended brain dendrites had been fully activated to receive the energy input of the Gamma Rays. Combined with this was the auto deactivation of his pineal gland converting his brain from a divided intuitive and analytical halves to a singularity pulsating and merging with an infinite potential reality of selfless being in total peace joy and harmony in an unbounded state of being as a thousand petalled lotus bloomed into nothingness. Later he would recall that he had not experienced this fullness but had actually become it. This was Dr Roy's vision and Charles had fructified it through technology. Man and nature had mated to procreate a transcended being heralding the onset of an 'era of truth' as Gopal would explain to Charles later. Kalyuga would evolve into Satyuga proving that Dysfunction was a prelude to metamorphosis. Science and Spirituality had merged to create a new MAN.

It was much later in the wee hours of the dawn that Charles left the lab enraptured by the techno mystic experience of the night and silently thanked Dr Roy for being his inspirational guide. As he entered his studio apartment in downtown Dubai there was only one word that he shouted out to himself at the top of his voice:

"EUREKA".

21

THE LORD'S LEELA

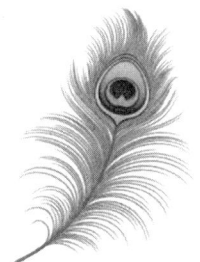

Adam was brilliant, affectionate and charismatic and lately meticulous enough to always err on the side of caution. Ever since his interaction with Dr. Roy he had grasped that the human mind continuously constructs a coherent picture of what is going on in our world. Often human preferences defy rationality. The key to controlling oneself was self observation or a continual surveillance of one's own mind and thoughts arising in it, as the Lama had once told him.

The media magnet was now fully aware of an intellectual self-growth that maybe would form a study launch pad for his current endeavors connected to Parvati, the human quest for excellence and higher evolution. The King of Global Media was at that point of time very much a part of Dr. Roy's team as the Lama had predicted the manifestation of chapter 19 of the Gita dynamic reality facilitating man's transcendence. The secret chapter would bloom into the open like a visible lotus from its hidden seed and catalyze the human race to new infinite heights of evolution. The mere thought of impending success thrilled him. Adam was a happy man.

Life is short they say but deep enough for grave lessons to be learnt. There is but one consolation. Love. True enchanting love engulfs silently but firmly with threads of pleasure that can snap but don't and make you bypass the irritants and traumas of life. It is a mental penetration based on the physical one and the orgasm lasts much longer. Adam knew he would always remain a flirt. The workable option would lie in changing the targets from multiple to singular and that too his one and only life partner. A satisfying grunt escaped from Adam as the thought that she would be joining him soon gently passed by like a French perfume. He then turned to the other serious matter and picked up the hotline to talk to the head of the Apps Section.

Dr. Roy had completed the research work at Dharamshala and would now coordinate with Adam and his App department to reach the winning point before the deadline of the Expo inauguration. The Begum would be co coordinating the peace offensive among nations from the expo venue. Parvati was busy in planning the media campaign to be launched by Adam's mega media house to cover the Expo globally. Gopal was acting like a shadow to Dr. Roy, always available and at his beck and call. Everyone was busy in their individual roles adding up to a grand design. Dubai would now form the hub for all activity till the expo, which was just 2 months away. The race had not only begun but was about to end. It remained to be seen

THE LORD'S LEELA

whether China would be contained on the one hand and whether Dr. Roy would be able to activate the secret chapter of the Gita on the other. In either scenario the epicenter would be the city of lights. It was symbolic that the tallest man made structure The Burj Khalifa would become the coordinate for the tallest human effort to uplift mankind to the highest level in human evolution.

Man was a minute but vital part of the Universe and Gopal had often wondered about the need for the creation of the human by the almighty infinite force and reached a conclusion that infinity cannot appreciate itself but can do so through a finite part created out of itself. The scriptures called it the 'Leela' or playfulness of the Lord. The Avatar of the Lord as Krishna was a reassurance to mankind that whenever evil raised its head the Lord would come.

The Tenth Avatar's appearance on earth would also mark the end of an era or 'Yuga'...the change over from 'Kalyuga' to 'Satyuga' from the era of deception to the era of truth. Gopal's mind was racing ahead now trying to keep pace with his thoughts. As per some ancient scriptures, the present Kalyuga would end and Satyuga would be starting in 2025. A gasp left Gopal's open mouth as he realized that it was now 2025. It also happened to be the year of the Expo.

That night in Dubai after a hectic day assisting Dr. Roy, acting as his personal aide, Gopal was staring at a birth chart spread before him. Astrological birth charts mapped the position of the planets at the time of a person's birth. In that sense Gopal viewed them like Google maps that were indicators of real situations. Of course the reader of such maps or charts played a crucial role in their reading. Gopal's thoughts were curtailed as his eyes focused on the astrological chart before him. He had only unraveled it with a partial glimpse of what it portrayed. Only time would confirm Gopal's vision. The horoscope would soon speak for itself.

It was that of Dr. Roy.

The Director was huddled together with the technical drones division at the CIA headquarters at Langley. The entire inside intel from Beijing was now available thanks to the CIA mole. The Chinese plan was truly sinister. The Presidents of America, Russia and France together with the Prime Ministers of Britain and India would be present at the inauguration of the Expo and their face, voice, genetic and 3D body makeup had been fed into the target details of the 5 drones to be launched from a Chinese region nearest to the Expo venue.

How the Chinese had got hold of such top classified data about the five leaders was a matter of a separate in-depth investigation. The drones were programmed to destroy the targets come what may and there would be no collateral damage. The upheaval caused in the major nations due to the vacuum in leadership executed simultaneously would give Beijing a head start to establish themselves as the undisputed global leader.

The Director had been baffled at first and was toying with the idea of advising the five leaders not to go to the Expo inauguration but then he knew the drones could still be used at separate locations to kill the leaders. The best way was to eliminate the drones from their control launch station itself. Tiger's team had come up with a brilliant modus operandi to do this and hence the briefing at Langley had become crucial.

Drones had initially started off as a harmless sophisticated toy. Around 2016 a multibillion-dollar Chinese manufacturer was selling 100000 drones monthly including online. This apparently harmless device coupled and developed through AI slowly became deadly weapons of killing termed 'slaughter bots' that used facial recognition to kill human targets before blasting their skulls.

Artificial intelligence had been developed and had been successfully introduced to some extent in most manufacturing, medical and service industries. The initial feedback was mixed with the vitality of continued human supremacy over intelligent robots still being adhered to. The introduction of AI in warfare was rather in its birth pangs.

In the circumstances, the meticulous and far reaching development of drone technology by the dragon nation did come as a surprise to Tiger personally.

The Director of the CIA was listening now with rapt attention to the presentation by his head of the hacking department. Cyber cum digital hacking technology had been developed by a leading US corporate but more recently a team from John Hopkins University had, using the digital deluge technology, confused launched drones to land thus saving the targets. The CIA researchers had carried this one step further. They had developed the expertise to land the drones and crash them at coordinates of their choice. The thought of crash landing the Chinese drones on Beijing itself amused The Director.

The CIA plan was simple but diabolic. The central computer at the Chinese Launchpad that would be the source of target profiling would be hacked an hour before the drones were to be launched to avoid detection. The CIA had a secret crack team of hacker experts who had assured Tiger they had done it before as a self-project and would guarantee a 100 per cent success rate for the current holocast. The drones and the profile data would be destroyed once and for all. The operation code named '5 Daggers' would be fatal for the dragon. The Director after a prolonged briefing of 4 hours finally appeared satisfied. He got an appointment with POTUS for that evening.

The only step that remained to save the world was a green signal from The White House.

22

THE REVELATION

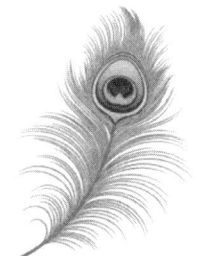

It is at rare moments that man's mind is capable of simultaneously experiencing a contradictory excursion that is both fascinating and frightening. It acts as a lucid, thorough and meticulous voice of consciousness that is distinctive and eloquent, blending deftly impending disaster with ultimate hope. Disaster like a cogent overview that is more terrifying because it is real based on a combination of massive natural and man-made forces driving creation over the brink. Hope that is at once inspiring, humbling and deeply necessary since it emanates from the stupendous entity called man who is the ultimate powerhouse of a rare resounding and awesome spirit of not only survival but a transcendent evolution personally endeavored to be crafted by the somewhat select pillars of human potential; one such amazing dynamic instances of homo-sapiens brilliance was called Dr. Laik K. Roy.

The learned neurologist was well aware of his awesome potential as well as occasional sheer laziness that acted as a speed breaker to a swift and spectacular streak of success. Over his adolescent years he had wonderfully worked upon this weakness with a dedicatedly disciplined approach. His earnest endeavors had been rewarded and today he represented a near perfect of the best self-distilled essence, humanity had to offer as one ode to the enigmatic force that had created in man a unique species of physical, mental and spiritual excellence that was not only endowed with the rare gift of self-awareness but as of date stood on the evolutionary edge of experiencing its own infinite creator.

Expo 2025 was almost at hand. Organized under the auspices of The Paris Convention, 200 nations would be putting up their pavilions towards showcasing their economic and cultural ethos. Millions would participate and billions of Dollars worth business would be transacted. Connecting minds and unlocking potentials through what promised to be a mega eco-social adventure of the globe. All important nations would be participating except one who had declined the invite. China.

Adam had got up abruptly that morning troubled by the irritating alarm. He knew he had to rush to the conference room in response to the Director Apps request made a day earlier that he wanted to communicate good news personally to the Chairman in the distinguished presence of Dr. Roy. He slipped out of his bed in the buff and straight in the washroom. The shower was invigorating but the sight of his athletic nude body in the full length mirror, forming one wall of the shower cabin, was even more so Narcissistic. Soon he was being driven in his latest Mercedes to attend and chair a

THE REVELATION

presentation that promised to be historic.

As he entered the presentation room with Crimson decor as per his liking for the king's colour, the top five of the company rose to greet the Chairman. The Chairman acknowledged the greetings but went straight towards Dr. Roy to vigorously shake his hands. Dr. Roy had arrived a minute earlier with Gopal and on seeing Adam spoke up in his casual voice:

"How have you been Adam?"

They then all settled down to witness the presentation by The Director Apps. The presentation started by explaining that the two primary methods to reach out and stimulate a human brain from inside normally was either through hearing or seeing. The Apps department of the mobile division had used and prepared an audio-visual App that if played at the required frequency would emanate gamma waves that would slowly penetrate into the human brain through the twin sensory perception inlets of sound and sight and using cellular micro-technology nullify the divisive role of the pineal gland and empower the open ended dendrites to be part of the vast cosmic consciousness thereby exponentially expanding the brain's consciousness to hitherto amazing frontiers of infinity.

The secret chapter of the Gita would thus unfold on the day of the expo inauguration when the new mobile with this latest App. would be released and distributed free to the assembled masses. This expo inauguration would be coinciding with availability of this magic gadget across the globe on an unprecedented scale free of cost. This was Adam's pay back to society. Krishna's gift to Arjun on the battlefield of Kurukshetra would now unfold to humanity on expo day courtesy Dr. Roy and his team together with Adam.

At the moment the presentation ended and everyone had gone for tea in the adjoining cafe, Gopal was alone in the presentation room. A sudden thought emerged from deep inside him and a wild ecstatic cry escaped from his mouth. He had just unraveled the awesome secret of his neurologist mentor's horoscope.

He now knew who Dr. Roy was...

It was an awesome experience to be in a trance and merge in an infinite consciousness and be aware of the experience after going through it. Of course once the peak is over it is a miraculous feeling of prolonged joy or 'Ananda' as the scripture would say...more like a continuous memory of pleasure felt momentarily. Dr Roy had tested out the App and knew they had succeeded to simulate the feeling of expanded consciousness for short periods, which was enough to bestow a transcendence boosting love and peace around oneself and in one self. The capacity of brain potential to think, intuit and absorb exponentially all, as an infinite singularity experience was exactly the crux revealed in the secret chapter of the holy Gita. They had done it. This was what Krishna had bestowed on the kneeling Arjuna at the battlefield of Kurukshetra and this was what would be bestowed to humanity by Dr. Roy shortly.

THE REVELATION

Adam was feeling ecstatic at the Apps success and was looking forward to the launch of the new brand of mobiles their group would be launching to coincide with the inauguration of the Expo. This mobile would have the App named OM, which would facilitate human transcendence. In his childlike excitement he rang up Begum and as she picked up he blurted out:

"Good morning mom...just wanted to share the good news of the App. we have done it with your blessings..."

The Begum blessed him but did not want to share the ominous Chinese threat that hung over them like a cloud. The inauguration of the Expo and the launch of the new brand mobile were both under threat, she knew. She had to maintain this secrecy for tactical reasons. As soon as their conversation was over she got another call. Dr. Roy too sought her blessings and shared how Parvati had become like a daughter to him. They promised to catch up soon. She had met Gopal too and it had been a mystical meeting as if she knew him already.

In him, she had that evening seen a glimpse of the son she never had. Sometimes nature plays games to make bonds without blood ties. Here was a full pseudo family in the making with Dr. Roy and The Begum as parent figures to Parvati and Gopal who now saw each other as siblings.

As the Begum put down the phone she recalled an important agenda. The Director CIA had requested her to be available for a conference call with POTUS regarding the security plan for the D-Day. She must go to her office immediately.

At the appointed time, The Begum was in her sound proof cabin talking to POTUS. He had news for her. The 5 leaders were in constant touch and had decided to attend the inauguration after POTUS had shared the CIA plan to eliminate the drones. The exact time of the CIA offensive would be disclosed to the leaders a day before the inauguration. The Begum closed the hotline with relief. Things appeared in control. Still something was bothering her deep down inside her and it would not go away soon she knew, the emotional fool that she knew she was.

The betrayal by Madame Lee would haunt her forever.

23

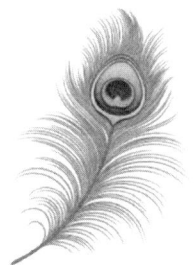

GOOD - THE ULTIMATE WINNER

It was the night before the Expo opening. That night Gopal and Dr Roy had an amazing interaction that they would remember for the rest of their lives. The clock had struck midnight and Gopal was engrossed in the study of planet movements depicted on the vast chart spread over his teak bed like a double bed spread. A vigil. That was what his eyes were conducting as he perused each corner of the vast planetary chart that night. A strange phenomena was in the making as Gopal scrutinized the central portion of the vast document. Gopal's grandfather had mentioned this phenomena only once to him in passing and it related to all the 9 planets coming in the same straight line axis—an extremely rare phenomena. After every few millennia the planets would be aligned and it would mark the advent of a new 'Yuga' or phase in the life of the Universe. His grandfather had further muttered some incoherent words so it was upto Gopal to solve the puzzle. Another look on his 'bedspread' and he got it. His stomach had started churning now. The planets were indeed aligning in a straight line already. There were the 4 ages and mankind stood at the threshold of 'Satyuga' or the era of truth. Gopal had already calculated the no of millenniums between each Yuga... A discreet knock and Dr Roy entered with two coffee mugs in hand as he remarked:

"Hi Gopal, could not sleep and seeing your light on, I walked in...care for some coffee..."

Gopal welcomed the offer as he commented:

"Dr Roy, I have been going through your astrological charts...would like to share something..."

The earlier bedspread was quickly replaced by a new chart. There were ten concentric circles emanating from Uranus at the centre, each circle representing a different lifetime of the subject. The distance between the concentric circles was the same in what appeared to Gopal to be in millenniums. The distance represented between two concentric circles would indicate after how many millennia Dr Rai would be reborn each time. The coffee tasted wow and Gopal said so. Gopal told Dr Roy that he would now proceed to measure the distance between two circles by a micrometer scale and asked Dr Roy to hold the chart steadily while he did so. The measured distance would then be factored by multiplying it by the scale adopted to reveal the number of millenniums between each rebirth of Dr Roy's soul. Gopal diligently measured while Dr Roy held the chart and soon calculated the desired millenniums. Both stood dumb struck staring at each other.

The gap in millennia between the heavenly planets

coming in a straight line was exactly the same as between Dr Roy's each rebirth on Earth repeated over and over again for ten different lifetimes.

The D-day was at hand. All the five top leaders had arrived the same morning and were booked into different hotels in the city. The strategy to have separate hotels for the leaders was deliberate from the security point of view. The various pavilions were all decked up in the traditional styles of the participant nations with a common hall of nations where the inauguration would take place. The host nation had made all arrangements for the Expo to be a grand success but Begum Bano knew of the danger fast approaching. She had already established direct contact with all the five top leaders and hotlines had been accordingly activated.

A call from The Director CIA to the Begum informed her of the exact time when the Chinese drones would be deactivated through the hacking process as planned. There was tension in the Begum's mind as she coordinated with the leaders. The inauguration of the phone app was also approaching and Adam was huddled with his staff for the detailed plan along with Dr. Roy and Gopal. Parvati was by Adam's side to assist him in any way required.

The American hackers were fully activated as per schedule. The experts had been able to penetrate right into the core of the launch procedures and were in a position to rewrite the programme that governed the destination of the drones. The head of the hacking team had earlier shared a brilliant thought with his colleagues and had also got permission from the Director to change the destination of the drones from the expo to the Chinese capital itself right into the headquarters of the Chinese Politburo. Normally it would not have been possible to stop a launch of these drones 100 times faster than human cognition with sensors and facial recognition.

It was only thanks to the mole who procured the password to tinker with launch instructions that had made this near miracle possible. Soon the time to redirect the drones would be at hand.

The Expo slogan 'Connecting Minds' was being displayed everywhere. At the stroke of the appointed hour the expert American hackers became suddenly activated. The leader of the team was now working furiously over the console in front of his workstation and simultaneously communicating with the other team members vocally through the speaker. The whole process of the American net offensive was being conducted well in advance of the launch time of the drones by the Chinese. It took them 28 minutes to enter, hack and exit from the Chinese launch website in such a perfect manner that when the Chinese launched the drones the drones would initiate the zoom from Central Asia towards Beijing. The second the American operation was done The Director was informed who in turn informed POTUS who in turn informed the assembled leaders at the expo. They all heaved a sigh of relief and now looked forward to the inauguration with a sense of safe pleasure and joy.

At that moment Adam and Dr Roy were shouting ecstatically on completion of the OM app. Parvati could not resist giving a kiss to Adam and a hug to Gopal who had joined them at that stage. The Begum sat in her private chamber waiting for an hour till the time to go to the inauguration came.

She was alone.

Praying.

The two hundred flags were fluttering merrily on the rather breezy but sunny day at the Expo venue. It was a day to be proud looking at the meticulous cooperation among the participating nations, especially the host country. The security was tight and fool proof. It was truly a grand spectacle and an awesome meeting of minds at display. Past experience combined with present action was combining to usher in an amazing future for mankind.

The leaders started arriving a few minutes before the inauguration with POTUS being the first to enter soon followed by the Russian President. They hugged each other warmly in full view of the masses. The events were being telecast globally live by Adam's mega media house. Within minutes all the leaders and the Begum were seated on their designated places on stage. The 5 leaders would shortly do the honours and would jointly inaugurate the Expo by pushing the 5 button switch of different colours, each leader handling one button. They would be seated on the dias along with the Begum and thousands of guests facing them along a vast oblong seating arrangement adjoining the Burj Khalifa.

It was on the top floor from Adam's office that the app OM would be launched and all the assembled guests and the general public would be given subsidized smartphones of the latest brand being assembled at Adam's organizational headquarters. At the appointed hour the Om App would become functional and the users would be able to experience a taste of transcendence. The vision of the secret and final chapter would soon be activated for man. Of course the assembled public did not still have the inkling about the Chinese menace and the fact that it had been contained hopefully. They would soon know.

The Begum was still somewhat tense.

She had been ushered onto the stage where she would be at the Centre stage along with the 5 leaders and was seated right next to POTUS. A brief whispered greeting was exchanged between the two. Both knew that the day was vital. Soon one by one the leaders spoke of unity and love among nations to ensure peace and progress on the globe. The National anthems of all participating nations were playing in the background. The crowds swelled. The time was approaching for the inauguration and the Chinese drone team were awaiting the green signal to launch.

At exactly the appointed time before the inauguration, the head of the Chinese launch gave the green signal to launch. A strange thing happened as the drones were launched...they zoomed towards Beijing instead of the leaders for whom they were meant. The head of the Chinese launch team let out a cry of despair. He was totally puzzled and helpless. At that very moment the leaders pressed their respective buttons and a massive shower of light and music signaled the Expo open amongst thunderous applause.

The atmosphere in Beijing was eerie as the drones approached. It was a low hum at first. Shaking the ground a bit un-gently and whispering into the ears of the unwitting populace of the city in an unshaken get monotonous tone. Every passing second saw the sound of doom grow like a whizzing of flaps through the air soon reaching a crescendo accompanied by a mega cloud of smoke.

Almost instantly, like an angered swarm of bees the cloud dissipated in the blink of an eye but the psychological damage to the dragon nation was complete as they realized that they had become their own target.

On top of the Burj Khalifa things were tense with anticipated excitement as the OM App was all set for the launch. Adam was busy directing his team with Parvati by his side.

Gopal was watching the learned neurologist who had a powerful glow on his face. He could see the masses assembled with the bright red cell phones being waved in the air awaiting activation. Gopal could intensely feel history in the making. The fulcrum moment of destiny when one era dies to give birth to another.

Dr. Roy at that moment was in deep thought as if an internal force was taking over his whole being. He suddenly experienced a divine light imploding inside him and dissolved his whole being even as he shouted out for the OM App to be launched.

24

THE TENTH AVATAR

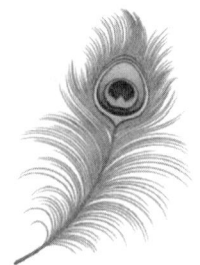

The Begum could well term her internal experience as ecstasy after the agony. There sitting on the crystal decorated stage along with the top 5 Global leaders was indeed ecstatic after days of agony caused by the dragon danger. Ever since changes in the U.N. charter doing away with the post of secretary general and delegating the functions to the Chairperson of the U.N. Development Foundation, Madame had done full justice to her global role. At that instant she knew she had achieved the Nobel Poet Tagore's Vision:

"Where the head is held high and the mind is without fear..."

Lucky are those whose personal and professional peaks of perfection coincide in life. The Begum was one of these. If at that point she thought she was to die, there would be no regrets. Her mental musings were cut short with a crisp announcement on the public address system:

"Ladies and Gentlemen, please standby for the launch of the OM App."

An air of tense expectancy prevailed upon the mammoth human gathering looking towards the tallest man-made structure on the globe, the Burj Khalifa, headquarters of the Global Media Inc., from where the launch would be made. The five leaders got up from their seats on stage, along with Begum and a thunderous applause spread like a virulent virus in anticipation of what was coming.

It was then that it happened.

The huge hologram in the sky lit up to announce the activation of the OM App.

This was history being born. The transformation of being to becoming. Gopal could feel the excitement in the infinite ocean of people attending the inauguration as Parvati was exchanging happy glances with him as her camera team caught the moment on camera. The free mobiles had already been provided to the population and would soon reach all corners of the globe. Adam had been a little silent but seeing the cameras beam the people's reaction as they switched on and experienced the OM App he knew they had done it. He rushed to Dr. Roy to hug him and convey his congratulations. Gopal then realized that Science and Spirituality had combined to grant a paradigm upliftment to humanity.

Adam was feeling rather ecstatic at the huge success of his team in developing the OM App. under the direction of Dr. Roy. Ever since Parvati had entered his life, luck had been ushered into his life accompanied by a stable variety of love in sharp contrast to momentary pleasure. She was truly his sole friend, philosopher and guide leading him on the right path. What a day it had been with his headquarters being the launching pad for a new beginning for man.

Dr Roy was like a halo of light it seemed to Gopal who was observing his mentor closely. The secret chapter of the Gita had come alive. The expressions of the people that had hooked on to the App were ecstatic as they felt their minds transcend the moment they hooked on to the App. Soon they would be able to do it naturally after practice and the experience would grant them peace and joy in the core of their expanded consciousness leading to peace and universal brotherhood. The era of Satyuga had begun. The eternal glimpses of the sacred secret had been achieved through the cosmic contact by removal of the black rainbow of evil.

Dr. Roy sub-consciously realized the significance of the dream he used to have often on being at a battlefield with two armies facing each other ready to engage in war but the fleeting thought was drowned in the pace of events being unfolded now. When the Lama had urged him to go on the Gita exploration, little did Dr. Roy imagine the awesome nature of the mission or the fact that one day he would succeed in that mission. The amazing activation of the vision of the secret 19th chapter of the Gita through his vital role was a fact that the Nobel neurologist was yet to fully grasp.

The whole of Adam's team had been invited to join the leaders on stage and as Dr. Roy met The Begum and all the 5 leaders the entire population gave them a standing ovation. A new chapter in human history had just started and the

THE TENTH AVATAR 153

evil Chinese menace had been defeated accompanied by a transcendence of humanity. Kalyuga was over and the new transcendence would usher in a revolutionary pure goodness, compassion and love in the human race. It was just as Krishna had told in the Gita. Gopal's mind was racing now. He had just remembered Krishna's promise to Arjuna that he would be there. It was precisely at that micro-moment that Gopal's eye fell on the majestic Dr. Roy the man who had made it all possible. Dr. Laik Roy. His first name LAIK...Gopal was laser like in his thinking now.

The alphabets in Dr. Roy's first name reshuffled threw up the word KALKI. This then was the 10th Avatar of Vishnu...Dr. Roy was Krishna himself fulfilling his Gita promise:

'I will be there'...

A fresh new dawn dawned the next morning on the globe after a full moon and man transcended to a new dimension in consciousness that acted as a catalyst for universal positive feelings of global brotherhood, truth, righteousness, love, and peace. It was as if humanity had experienced a spiritual orgasm. The OM App spread globally like an awesome victory virus which wood kick start mankind towards an auto new Avatar. Kaliyuga was over and had handed the baton to Satyuga. The book of time had flipped a page and a new era had begun.

That morning the Begum had organized a prayer at her home and everyone was ecstatic to be together. Gopal was over busy making all the arrangements. Adam and Parvati were to be wed and The Begum along with Dr Roy would be the girl's parental figures while Gopal fitted into a brother's role automatically. It was like a small family gathering. Adam of course looked resplendent as the bridegroom flirting with Parvati even during the wedding ceremony.

Parvati's wedding was indeed a joyous culmination to the recent somewhat turbulent local scenario. What was incredulous was the release of the secret 19th chapter of the Gita to mankind and in a most spectacular manner through the OM App. Launch. A sparkling knowledge under wraps for millennia had now been presented to humankind empowering a momentous paradigm shift in man's evolutionary journey to a higher dimension. An amazing overlap in some personal lives had unfolded a historic cosmic destiny. That was how nature worked through its own creation called life. An infinite intelligent force had created the universe and put a cherry called man on the cake. Surreptitiously and steadily, this human self-aware jewel of the Universe had begun the return journey towards experiencing the infinite, the powerful and the super intelligent energy source of its own creation and maybe over the coming millenniums ultimately merge in it completely.

Gopal was unable to sleep that night as he relived the moments from the revelation of the existence of the secret chapter to its activation for humanity. The divine vision stood fulfilled.

Krishna's promise to man stood redeemed.

25

Transcendence

As Dr Roy's Uber cab approached the outskirts of Dharamshala, he felt virtually lost in his exotic surroundings. Looming over the skycap was the towering mountain rising abruptly from the blanket of snow with its jagged crags and serrated cliffs shaping the mound of rook into a razor sharp tiger tooth piercing the heavens above. A circlet of wispy clouds surrounded the high peak affirming the title 'the Unconquered'. Peppering the surroundings were its subordinates, their attempt to reach ever closer to the azure sky paling in comparison to the leader. Heart thudding in anticipation at the fervent beat of a hundred drums.

The Lama welcomed Dr Rai personally amidst the drum beats. Gopal had already arrived and warmly touched his mentor's feet. A week had elapsed since the release of the Om App. and a sense of deep ecstasy, peace and progress had been engulfing humanity around the globe as witnessed by the headlines. The wisdom was based on actual experience of an evolution tantamount to transcendence. All beings felt connected with the feeling of oneness. The parameters of commerce and personal ethics changed. Deceit hatred jealousy cheating selfishness violence became extinct as the realisation of one-ness dawned on the globe.

Soon enough a monk of tender age announced more guests and in walked Adam, Parvati and the Begum. The chorus was complete. The session of green tea was joyous as the Lama announced that henceforth all Published copies of the Gita would carry 19 Chapters. Parvati announced that Adam had made a TV film on their journey of seeking the secret chapter and the Om App with its global aftermath. The premiere was to be telecast in an hour's time.

Soon they were all stationed in the Lama's private auditorium. As the film commenced the title in bold letters filled the screen. It read:

"The Gita Secret".

A few years later...

Gopal is visiting Dubai and rings up Parvati and she invites him for dinner. The door is opened by a maid and he is ushered into a large dining room. The chattering of two kids greets him. Parvati and Adam now have a boy of 5 and a girl of 3. They hug him and are delighted to meet Uncle Gopal. The names of the kids enthrall him—Aaditya and Aditi. He has kept the names being astrologically auspicious. As he leaves, Adam hugs him and Parvati too with the kids kissing him endlessly. A strong bond. In the temple room, he has seen two garlanded pics of Dr. Roy and Begum Bano. Time must go on and he must reach the pinnacle of astrology to redeem his grandfather's vision. He is on the right track as testified by his insight that moment when he is leaving Parvati's home. Aaditya and Aditi cling to him tightly to bid goodbye.

It is at that moment that he knows that Dr. Roy and Begum Bano still live...

Epilogue

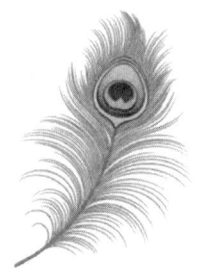

One month after the drones fiasco, the Chairman of the People's Republic of China has summoned Lady Lee to his private office. The conversation runs thus.

The Chairman: Lady, I have called you for a vital mission. You are directed to proceed to Wuhan Institute of Virology and take over as The Chief Controller of the secret Bio-terror wing of the institute. I am informed that the covert research mission to develop an artificial now deadly virus has reached a vital stage, together with a vaccine to protect-our own nation. We propose to unleash this bio bomb globally at selected enemy targets within the year under your leadership. The mission is code named CORONA 2025. Please proceed immediately to Wuhan and await further instructions.

Lady: Respected Chairman Sir, I am truly honored and shall leave immediately.

Madame Lee bows and respectfully takes leave of the Chairman.

A new challenge awaits humanity...